Week Ending is Radio 4's topical comedy show with a regular cult audience, not all of whom have tuned in too early for the Shipping Forecast. It has been running for five years longer than Lord Lucan.

Ian Brown resigned from the Ministry of Agriculture in 1982 when the tension of high-level politics – writing the house journal – led him to seek less strenuous employment. However, due to misinformation he became a full-time scriptwriter for "Week Ending". In 1984 the Ministry noticed that he had gone. Recently he has acquired his first flat, in London's Queen's Park, but the AA say that they'll be along shortly. Ian is married to his work; at the moment they are receiving Guidance. His hobby is writing application forms to rejoin the Civil Service.

James Hendrie decided to offer his brain to the country after its three-year rest at Cambridge (Emmanuel College III, with Sylvia Kristel). On getting it back with a rejection slip he took instead to offering sketches to the BBC, which were warmly accepted, together with the postal orders he enclosed along with them. Excluding monthly breaks to write funeral orations for members of the Politburo, he has held the position of a "Week Ending" scriptwriter since 1981. He and Ian are at present writing a six-part silent movie for Radio 4.

Week Ending: The Cabinet Leaks

Ian Brown & James Hendrie

With contributions from
Martin Booth, David Cohen, Paul B. Davies,
Jeremy Hardy, John Langdon, Richard Quick,
Stuart Silver, Pete Sinclair, Mike Coleman
and John Pye

Sphere Books Limited
London and Sydney

Week Ending is a BBC Radio 4 programme featuring
Bill Wallis, David Tate, Sally Grace and Jon Glover

First published in Great Britain by
Sphere Books Ltd 1985
30-32 Gray's Inn Road, London WC1X 8JL

Conceived and produced by Adamson Books
By arrangement with the British Broadcasting Corporation
Illustrations by Jonathan Inglis,
Steve Cross, Ian Brown and James Hendrie

Special thanks to the *Week Ending* producers –
Jennie Campbell, Paul Mayhew-Archer and Paul Spencer;
to Mary Bell, Jane Bell, Max Alcock and Peter Hickey

Photographs have been kindly supplied by: BBC Hulton Picture Library, British Railways Board, Camera Press (Jon Blau, Philippe Boucas, Peter Francis, Ray Green, Steven Lundstrom, Michael Palladin, Norman Sagansky, Geoffrey Shakerley), City Syndication, Joris, The Kobal Collection, Popperfoto, Christopher Smith, Topham Picture Library, Thorn – EMI, The Whitehall Mole

Typeset by Wagstaffs Design Associates
Reproduced, printed and bound in Great Britain by
Hazell, Watson & Viney Limited, Aylesbury, Bucks
ISBN 0-7221-4782-1

Foreword by the Rt. Hon. Margaret Thatcher M.P.

Prime Minister and First Lord of the Treasury, Empress of India, Master of the Galaxy, Mekon of Mekonta

YOU KNOW, I didn't need to be asked twice to write the foreword to this book. In fact, I wasn't asked once. But I became convinced that my writing it was the correct thing to do the moment my advisers told me not to.

Funnily enough, I'm often accused of not having a sense of humour. Far from it. I think laughter is the sugar on the bitter and very large pill you've jolly well go to take to set Britain back on its stumps – even if I have to blow it up your backsides with a jet of compressed air. Yes, we need laughter to help us through this nation's dark and difficult days (e.g. when I'm away on holiday). And if more levity were needed, just think of our great achievements after a mere six and a half years in office – democracy in Argentina and inflation almost down to what it was when we took over.

I think I should at this stage say that I'm not a big book person. Give me a densely written file on Concrete, Aggregates and Related Building Materials any day, but I'm told this book is a "light read", so I expect it's along the lines of the Report on the Proceedings of the Environmental Committee on Permitted Emulsifiers.

Reading through the book, you may come across contributions from some of my subordinates, or "colleagues" as my press office likes me to call them. They're all doing such a marvellous job that I have no intention of removing any of them from office, but if I do, see below.

Yours in a sincere whisper,

Margaret Thatcher

MARGARET THATCHER

IN CASE OF RESHUFFLE –
CUT OUT AND PASTE OVER THROUGHOUT THE BOOK

DHSS

HOME SECRETARY

DEFENCE

ANYTHING

WHITEHALL CLAMPS DOWN

Next week the *New Statesperson's* cover price goes up to £1.47. In order to justify this we publish here a series of remarkable documents which DUNCAN CAMPBED unearthed while reading last week's *Guardian*.

10 October 1983

Dear Margaret
You remember when we fiddled the rules a bit so we could sink that overgrown Wop bathtub [SS *General Belgrano*]? Well, Tampax Dan [*Tam Dalyell M.P.*] is making such a bloody nuisance of himself [*asking questions in the House*] that it could lead to further tragedy [*loss of the next election by the Conservative Party*]. So I'm going to pretend it never happened and feed the House of Commons with a lot of duff gen. Is this all right?

Yours
Mike [*Heseltine*]

PS I hope nobody leaks this!

12 October 1983

Dear Michael
Thank you for your letter of 10th October, which I received on page 3 of the Guardian. I wish you wouldn't refer to them as Wops. Ethnographically they are in fact Dagoes. And it's *Mr* Tampax to you.

Yours
Elizabeth R.
[Rt Hon. Margaret Thatcher M.P.]

PS It's OK about telling whoppers to the House!!!

3 December

Dear Margaret
You know, I've got a funny feeling that some of our correspondence has been slipping out. I only say this because my PPS, Driver, Tea Lady and the entire canteen staff have just joined the NUJ. By the way, Sir Geoffrey Ho[*we*]rlicks says his clerks insist that the photocopying machine round there has broken and can only do 200 copies at a time.

Yours
Mike

PS Funny old world, isn't it?

19 December 1983

Dear Michael
Thank you for your most recent letter, 200 copies of which I found blowing down Whitehall. What do you mean it's a funny old world? I don't find it particularly funny. Except when a dog gets run over.

Yours
Boudiccaa

PS Do something about the leaks or the old guy [*Viscount Whitelaw*] gets it.

15 January 1984

Dear Margaret
I think I have the answer. All we have to do is write in code and then no-one will understand what we're nm zants. Cn xnt rdd? Hs'r rn rhlokd! Sgzs'r qhfgs--H'l vqhshmf hm bncd mnv!

Yours
Mike www

8 Edaqtzqx

Dear Michael
Xibu b tqmfoeje qmbo! J'n xbtujoh op sjnf qvuujoh ju jmup bdujpo, bt zpv dbo tff!

Zpvst
Jmtb

37 49012

Dear 46213
67279 63612 51916 72988 48390 00982 35567!!

Yours
64197
PS What is it you're trying to say?

4 August 1984

Dear Mike
I think we'd better drop the code idea.

Yours
Messalina

PS Can't tell you. It's a secret!

3 September

Dear Margaret
Agreed. But you'll be pleased to hear (a) That your letters are being serialised in the *Observer*, and (b) we've tracked down the source of the leaks. We think it's a Civil Servant called Clive Ponting! [No it bloody isn't – CP]

Yours
Mikey Boy

PS I suppose somebody's head will have to roll for this? How about Geoffrey's?

URGENT TELEX

FROM DEFHEAD 3.09.1984

TO PRIMECON

THE BIT IN MY LAST LETTER ABOUT GEOFFREY'S HEAD ROLLING WAS A JOKE. DO YOU UNDERSTAND? A JOKE. LIKE EDWARD HEATH.

17 November

Dear Michael
Thank you for your letter, which didn't reach me before it had been made into a transparency and projected onto the clouds above London. As for the urgent telex unfortunately it arrived while I was in the Far East but Madame Tussaud's have stepped into the breach with a replacement.

Yours
Maria-Christine de Lalaing [*Look it up*]

PS Is Edward Heath a joke? I didn't know he was ill.

22 December

Dear Margaret
Thanks for your letter. Somebody called Puttnam has approached me about the film rights. About the leaks – Geoffrey and I thought it would be a good idea to give those members of staff who had leaked things a chance to own up by signing a written confession. So we are a bit snowed under with paperwork at the moment.

Yours etc

PS We can't pin anything on Ponting so suggest we do him under the Official Secrets Act.

3 January 1985

Dear etc
Agreed. Though Havers tells me the best we can do under the Act is two years for leaking documents and seven years for embarrassing me. Can't we do him for something else? How about "Encompassing the death of the heir to the throne"?

Yours
Jane Eyre

PS Ha!

31 January 1985

Dear Margaret
For god's sake, Jane Eyre is a fictional character! Do you want to end up with them taking your shoelaces away? Ponting case fixed for Tuesday, Tower Hill.

Yours
Indiana Jones

PS Interesting counter-bid from Warner Bros.

7 February 1985

Dear Indy
Shame about Ponting getting off. Has the whole world gone mad or is it me?

Yours
Hahahahaha.
PS Burblurblurlbur.

8 February

Dear M
It's you.

Yours
Q

PS Defence spending could do with an extra boost next year so suggest we prepare the ground in the usual way. You know – put a list of our naval deficiencies in a plain brown envelope to the *Telegraph*.

12 February

Dear Q
What happened about the whoppers?

X.

4 Thermidor

Dear X
I think we got away with it.

Z.
PS I think there's something you should know about our phone tapping cover-up.

STATE OF LEBANON

PRIME MINISTER

A vacancy keeps arising at the head of the Lebanese government. Applications are welcomed from suitably qualified candidates with a practical interest in the afterlife.

No experience necessary. No political skill necessary. Tin hat essential. Applicants intending to find their own accommodation should also have a qualification in Archaeology.

The successful candidate's work will fall into three main sections, but then so do most things round here. First, you will be expected to lead your people (subject to their availability). Secondly, you will receive frequent visits from foreign diplomats: the entire Israeli Army. Your third duty is to rally the opposing factions within the Lebanon behind a common goal – getting rid of you.

Operating in a fast-changing environment, indeed building, you will be working directly under the President – because he's fallen through the ceiling.

Driving licence (tank) would be an advantage.

Salary: 13,000 rounds (please state whether .38 or .45).

For application form and further details, send SAE to:
3rd hole on the left, Rubble House, Beirut; if not there try Red Cross Tent.

The State of Lebanon is an Equal Opportunities Employer – we don't care who gets the job.

BUCKINGHAM PALACE

Dear Mr. Milne. Here's the Xmas spiel you asked for on the dog and bone. I've tried to make it a bit less controversial this time. Cheers EIIR

ADDRESS TO THE COMMONWEALTH BY HER MAJESTY QUEEN ELIZABETH II
BALMORAL CHRISTMAS 1985

Hullo. Happy Christmas. Well, the family and me have just had a jolly good pork-out I can tell you! And while the others are sleeping off the brandy butter in the Waterloo Room, I've just slipped away for a world wide telecast. It's been quite a year for the Commonwealth, Beirut, and Northern Ireland, hasn't it? But never mind that now. I hope Santa brought you everything you wanted. He brought me two thirds of Scotland and a box of After Eight. And Charles was well chuffed with his Neddie Seagoon mask! When he put it on, Philip joked: "Who are you? Get off my property". We were all in stitches. Charles was as thoughtful as ever – he gave Diana a nice bottle of "pong" and got his Auntie Margaret a Tom Caxton Home Brew Beer Kit. Anne was so hard to please last year we clubbed together and got her Boots voucher for £1.50. Anyway, I musn't hang about! We've been asked over for sherry by the next-door neighbours, and as they're twenty-five miles away we'd better get cracking!

But before I go, I'd like to read you this thought for the festive season: What happens when a duck flies upside down? Answer: He quacks up!!! Chin! Chin!

Got this from a cracker. Hope you can clear copyright!

E

SPINACH FLAN

AB '85 THE NEWSLETTER OF THE ANIMAL LIBERATION FRONT AB.'85

Dear Members (or should I say "Tendrils"!)

What a lot has happened since I last sopke to you! Last w eek we firebombed Mac-Fisheries, picketed Professor Marvo's Flea Circus and released over 1000 turkeys in Epping Forest. Latest reports say they8re defrosting nicely. Well done, Paul and Julie!

Meanwhile, the boycott of Peter Dominic, Maidstone continues. If, as the manager claims, it is made of grapes, why the Hell is it called "Bull's Blood"? But on a lighter note, the tension mounts vis à vis the kidnapping of the Haringey butcher's entire stock of meat. Make no mistake, brothers, sisters and planet-sharers, each day he refuses to pay the ransom, we're sending him another chipolata.

On Sunday we had a very successfullliberation in Battersea Park. Now at last our children can play happily among some of Nature's finxest creations - Minks, Tree Frogs, Scorpions. Not so successful was longstanding member Bill Chainstich's expedition to recruit the Lions of Longleat to the Cause of vegetarianism. The memorial service is on Tuesday.

At the Monthly General Meeting last week, Sophie Fennel made a stirring speech in favour of reforming our language. "Why" she asked, "do so many of our proverbs and sayings appear to condone meat eating and related activities?" She cited th e case of the expression, "more than one way to skin a cat". Well, if it's true, somebody must have tried it out. (Any info on his identity to me, please). She wnet on to suggest a few altenrative proverbs - "curiosity mashed the potato", "cat got your lettuce?" and "embarrasing two birds with one whoopee-cushion". Good for you, Sophe!

A vigorous discussion ensued in which it was proposed that in future our "night swoop" balaclavas should notbe made with animal products but knitted from the stringy bits in celery. Field trials are now progressing smoothly although Andrea Wholeweat was chased by a bunch of hungry rabbits into a duck pond. Nothing like dropping in on friends, Andrea(!)

And here are two dates for your diary. The 20th sees the Annual Pelting of the Minister of Agriculture (free-range eggs only, please!). And on the 23rd it's the assassination of Robert Carrier.

Finally, we8ve just heard some bad news from Battersea Park. The minks have eaten the tree frogs and the scorpions have killed the minks, but it's just Nature taking its course, isn't it?

WELL, I See the bottom of the page looming again, so it's time for me to sya "Soya soon!"

ANDY BEARDMORE, Chief Armadillo

PS. Remember, if you catch anyone abusing an animal, rip the fucker's head off.

Sir ▬▬▬
Chairman of British Rail

"British Rail Serves You Right" ⇌

A personal message from the chairman

"We at British Rail have been working hard to make our services more streamlined, competitive and cost-effective within the Government's annual financial target of £5.62. Naturally this has meant some administrative fine-tuning – like flogging off four thousand miles of track and sacking all the staff. But we have made some amazing technological advances, like the Supa-trak Futuro-Train, and Northern Ireland's own De Lorean Expressway. So I think you'll find there have been a number of improvements. If you do, please tell me where they are. Remember, this is truly the Age of the Train! Oh...I think I can hear my car...."

CHAIRMAN

PADDINGTON – SLOUGH – READING – ▬▬▬
SLOUGH – HALF WAY BACK TO READING –
SLOUGH – SLOUGH – SLOUGH – DIDCOT

SATURDAYS	ac	b	cd	gh	f
Paddington	10.31	......	......	......	....
Westbourne Park	......	......	......	......	....
Acton Main Line	......	......	......	......	....
Ealing Broadway	......	......	......	......	....
West Ealing	......	......	......	......	....
Hanwell	......	......	......	......	....
Southall	......	......	......	......	....
West Drayton	......	......	......	11.42	....
Iver	......	......	......	11.46	....
Twyford	......	......	......	......	....
Reading	......	......	......	......	....
Tilehurst	......	......	......	......	....
Pangbourne	......	......	......	......	....
Cholsey	......	......	......	......	....
Didcot	Thursday		......	......	....

- a Change at Hanwell
- b Change at Slough
- c Hang around at Slough for an hour
- d Change at Maidenhead
- e Spend three hours in a siding near Taplow
- f Change at Reading
- g West Drayton and Iver Thunderbolt Special
- h Change of clothing needed

While every effort is made to ensure that the information in this guide is accurate and up to date, the publishers cannot undertake responsibility for errors or omissions, lies, wilful deceit or sheer bloody-mindedness. And the several transport authorities do not guarantee arrivals or departures at the times stated, or indeed at any other time. Passengers may experience some delay or inconvenience as a result, but quite frankly, we couldn't give a toss.

ENQUIRIES (01) 246 8021 (24-hour ringing tone)
OR 33 Kookaburra Curve, Wagga-Wagga, New South Wales. (Personal Callers Only)

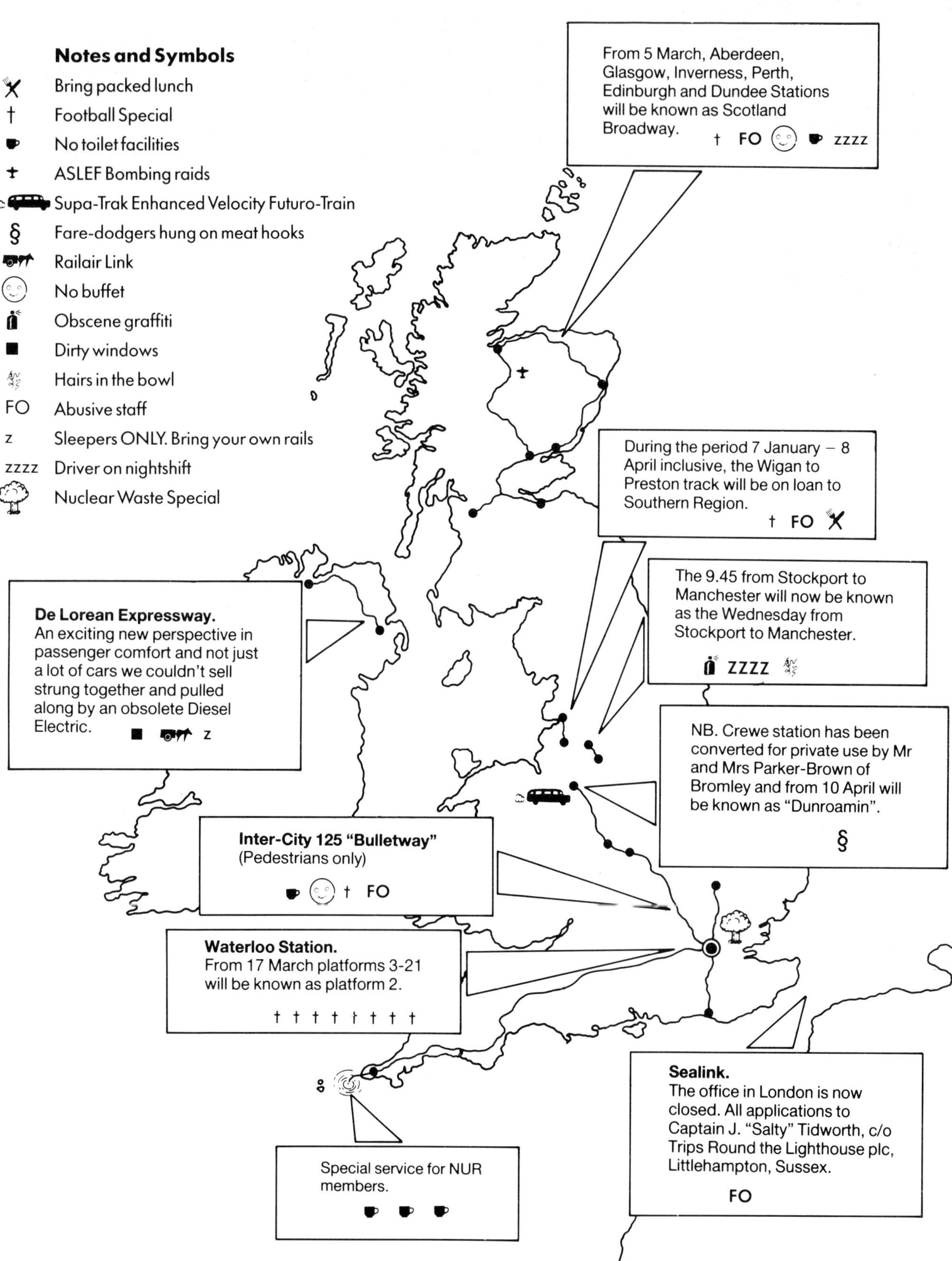

Notes and Symbols
Bring packed lunch
Football Special
No toilet facilities
ASLEF Bombing raids
Supa-Trak Enhanced Velocity Futuro-Train
§ Fare-dodgers hung on meat hooks
Railair Link
No buffet
Obscene graffiti
Dirty windows
Hairs in the bowl
FO Abusive staff
z Sleepers ONLY. Bring your own rails
zzzz Driver on nightshift
Nuclear Waste Special
From 5 March, Aberdeen, Glasgow, Inverness, Perth, Edinburgh and Dundee Stations will be known as Scotland Broadway.
† FO zzzz
During the period 7 January – 8 April inclusive, the Wigan to Preston track will be on loan to Southern Region.
† FO
The 9.45 from Stockport to Manchester will now be known as the Wednesday from Stockport to Manchester.
ZZZZ
NB. Crewe station has been converted for private use by Mr and Mrs Parker-Brown of Bromley and from 10 April will be known as "Dunroamin".
§
De Lorean Expressway.
An exciting new perspective in passenger comfort and not just a lot of cars we couldn't sell strung together and pulled along by an obsolete Diesel Electric.
z
Inter-City 125 "Bulletway"
(Pedestrians only)
† FO
Waterloo Station.
From 17 March platforms 3-21 will be known as platform 2.
† † † † † † † †
Sealink.
The office in London is now closed. All applications to Captain J. "Salty" Tidworth, c/o Trips Round the Lighthouse plc, Littlehampton, Sussex.
FO
Special service for NUR members.

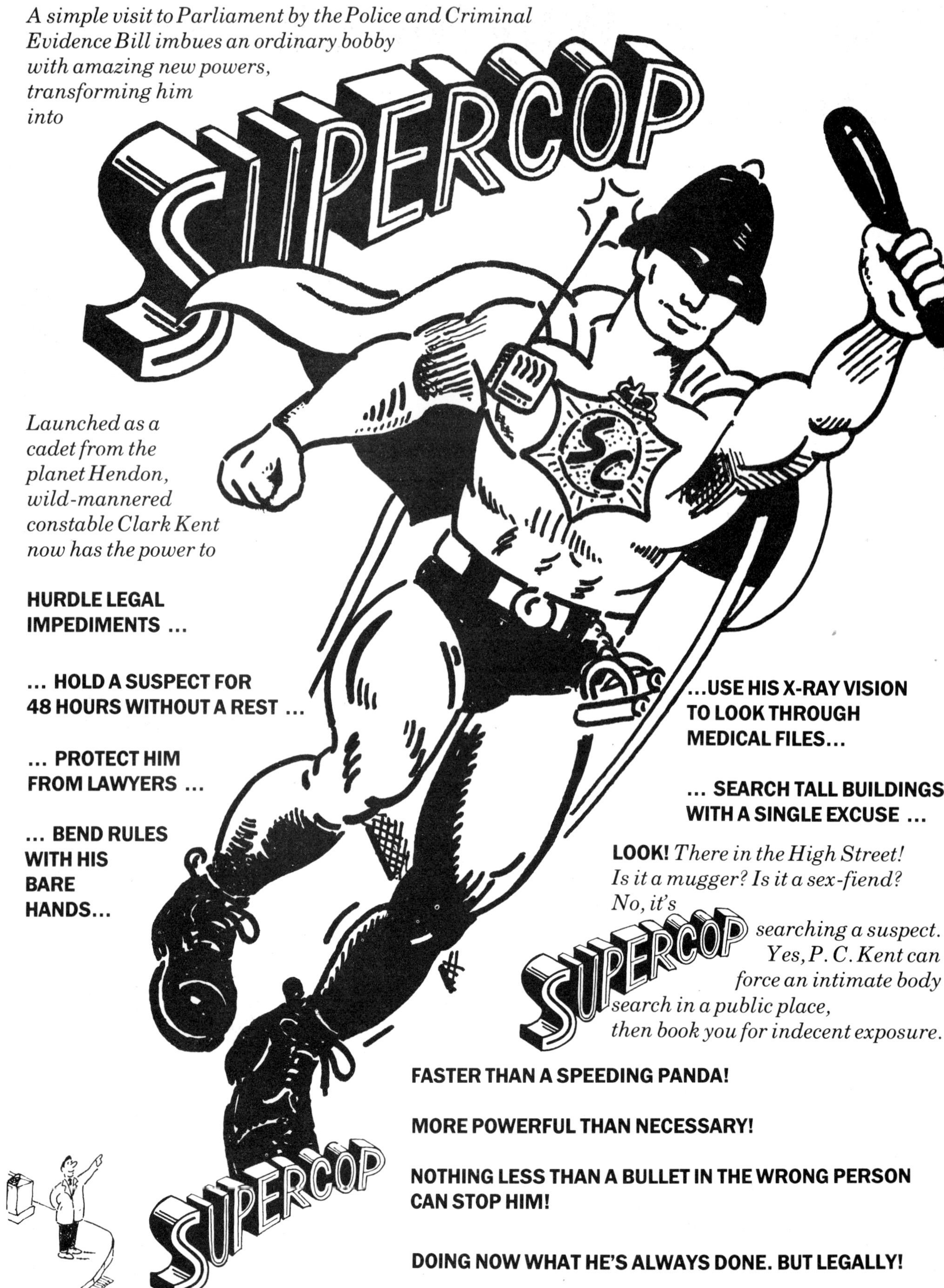

A simple visit to Parliament by the Police and Criminal Evidence Bill imbues an ordinary bobby with amazing new powers, transforming him into
SUPERCOP
SC
Launched as a cadet from the planet Hendon, wild-mannered constable Clark Kent now has the power to
HURDLE LEGAL IMPEDIMENTS ...
... HOLD A SUSPECT FOR 48 HOURS WITHOUT A REST ...
... PROTECT HIM FROM LAWYERS ...
... BEND RULES WITH HIS BARE HANDS...
...USE HIS X-RAY VISION TO LOOK THROUGH MEDICAL FILES...
... SEARCH TALL BUILDINGS WITH A SINGLE EXCUSE ...
LOOK! There in the High Street! Is it a mugger? Is it a sex-fiend? No, it's
SUPERCOP
searching a suspect. Yes, P. C. Kent can force an intimate body search in a public place, then book you for indecent exposure.
FASTER THAN A SPEEDING PANDA!
MORE POWERFUL THAN NECESSARY!
NOTHING LESS THAN A BULLET IN THE WRONG PERSON CAN STOP HIM!
SUPERCOP
DOING NOW WHAT HE'S ALWAYS DONE. BUT LEGALLY!

This Year, Why Not Choose A Holiday in Britain?

RAF
BRIZE NORTON

ASCENSION

Come to the **The Falklands**, Britain's very own off-shore paradise – where every Islander is a millionaire tax exile. Yes! The taxpayer spent a million on each of them and exile's where they're bloody staying.

We've got everything the Costa Brava's got:

- Horrible pubs
- Drunken Englishmen
- Brawls
- Reliable Weather

BUT NO DAGOES!

There's plenty to see on the twin pearls of the South Seas. (For more information send for our free brochure, The Official Secrets Act.)

You can go on safari and spot these rare breeds: The Charbroiled Sheep, The One-Winged Puffin, The Native Falklander.

Or see the womenfolk show their skills, such as evading the clutches of the local squaddies.

For your ease and safety:

Street map of Port Stanley

HOW TO GET THERE

Getting there's simple now we've completed the new airport at Mount Pleasant. However, if you find £4000 a flight too much to pay, it's possible to get Government help with the fare (details from your local Army Careers Office).

HMS
HERMES

MOUNT
PLEASANT
AIRPORT

HMS
INVINCIBLE

FALK-AIR serves more destinations in the South Atlantic than any other airline!
FLY THE FLAK!

Examine our Duty-Free Range:

Beers and Spirits
Sheepeater Gin
Scotch of the Antarctic
Goose Green Chartreuse
Penguinness
Sheep's Navy Rum

Perfume
Falklands Factor
Max Hastings
Brut Force

Tobacco
John Player Special (Air Service)
Sovrantie Cockup Cigarettes
Players' No.3 Para

Gifts
Sprig o' Lucky Kelp
Sony Yompman
Sundry Argie Memorabilia – Revolvers, Helmets, Limbs, etc.

Some of the Airport's Features

- Moving Walkway – There are still a few mines to be cleared
- VIP Lounge – (Sir Rex Hunt Only)
- International Phone Box – Insert a written request and allow 3 weeks to book your call
- AND REMEMBER: Mount Pleasant Airport boasts the Falkland Islands' most welcoming sight – the departure lounge

**THE FALKLANDS,
A HOME 8,000 MILES
FROM HOME**

CHAPTER VIII

WHEREIN NICHOLAS CONFRONTS SIR KEITH WACKFORD-SQUEERS, AND ENGAGES IN COMBAT OF A MENTAL NATURE.

IT WAS WITH NO LITTLE FEAR AND TREPIDATION that Nicholas entered the inner sanctum of his mentor; owner of Dotheboys Hall—Sir Keith Wackford-Squeers—whom he discovered placidly chewing a freshly buttered slice of Axminster.

"Ah, Nickleby!" said the pedagogue, sitting up sharply in his moleskin strait-jacket. "You have been stirring my masters up to revolt, have you not?"

"Indeed, sir," rejoined the other with strong emotion, "I must protest. The conditions we work in are intolerable. The classrooms are reminiscent of the workhouse and there is Disruption, Division and Despair in the classes."

"What!" exclaimed the schoolmaster with a violent swivel of the eyes that alarmed even such a seasoned interlocutor as Nicholas. "What! Show me the boys responsible for this and I'll thrash them to within an inch of their lives!"

Nicholas wiped a fleck of foam from his greatcoat. "It's not the boys, sir," he said, "it's the masters. Wait till I tell you how the boys feel."

"Enough, Nickleby!" ejaculated Squeers. "What is the cause of this unrest?"

"Sir Keith, the teachers need more money," came the reply.

"What?" The schoolmaster manoeuvred himself into such a position that he could eye both Nickleby and the green giraffe which he perceived was making its entrance by the casement. "But I already pay them a whole shilling a year."

"They need more," urged Nicholas, emboldened by his success in inveigling Sir Keith into negotiations.

"What do you think I am? Made of shillings?" said Squeers.

"Sir, for all their qualification and dedication they receive nary as much as a traffic beadle!" cried Nicholas in a towering passion.

"Well then, Nickleby," said Sir Keith, as the crack between his nose and chin contorted into that vague supposition of a smile normally associated only with the visits of his therapist, "I suppose you're right." But before the young man could savour the triumph welling in his breast Sir Keith continued: "Sack the teachers and get me some traffic beadles."

"But, sir," Nicholas remonstrated, "the masters put in so much voluntary work!"

"I thought you said I paid them?" said Sir Keith.

"Some of them are taking lessons out of school hours for no money at all!" replied Nicholas, mindful of his own attempts to master the extra-curricular class in woodwork, music, and lion-taming.

"Then this must be remedied," said Sir Keith, sending another surge of hope through the other man's soul. "Cancel all the scheduled lessons and continue all the voluntary ones!"

Nicholas's wrath was now thoroughly invoked, and he vented his fury at that despised pate that was now banging itself calmly against the study's exquisite Queen Anne padding.

"It is exactly that sort of attitude which is tearing Dotheboys apart!" cried Nicholas. "The masters are becoming depressed and disorientated, they are fearful and upset...your strategy, sir—it is driving them mad."

"I know," said Sir Keith, addressing not Nickleby but the purple hippopotamus that had just occupied the intervening space. "Perhaps then they'll see things from my point of view."

1. ON THE SCENT

THE NAME'S SPENCER, Private Investigator. I'd been hired by Derby Council to get the filth off the sidewalks and back into the gutter where it belonged. But it wasn't people dropping litter they wanted me to investigate. It was their sidekicks, dogs, unleashed on to parks and playgrounds to do their stinking business. This muckraking wasn't the kind of work I was used to but the council figured I had a nose for the job.

I was on the scent of a low-down sonofabitch, Jack Russell. I was going to do more than rub his face in the dirt. I was on his tail and I reckoned he'd make the drop. He had hard evidence but he was stoolie and I figured he'd loosen up.

But he was always too quick for me. I was getting nowhere fast. Then one day I realized I was right on top of what I was looking for. This time I was really in the evidence. The council had told me to step on it but this was ridiculous. I figured at least they wouldn't have me on the carpet. As it turned out, they wouldn't even have me in the building.

So here I am, all washed up. The council got rid of me. A guy who'd tried to get rid of something for them. I felt that I'd been treated like some piece of

WHODUNNIT!

PAKISTAN STAR

Ziaday, Ziauary 21, 1985	Published in ISLAMABAD Written by UL-HAQS	5 Rupees

Foreign News
Reagan appoints Satan as Foreign advisor. **p.5**

Holiday Page
This week: Ramadan. **p.7**

Put it to Zia
His Extreme Severity answers your complaints. Remember to enclose your full name and an address where you can be tracked down. **p. 8-9**

Agony Column
Round-up of this week's court cases. **p.10**

Books
Interview with Mohammed ul-Wazuq, veteran shop-lifter about his best-selling autobiography, "Look, Ma – No Hands!" **p.12-13**

Women's Page
Stop reading the paper and get on with the housework, you hussy.

Laugh with MEC

GENERAL ELECTED!

ZIA TOPS THE OPPOSITION

Early this morning the people of Pakistan were telling one another that the country had a new government. It didn't, but anyone who pointed this out had their testicles tied to a train. It's all part of the vigorous Islamic Constitution promised by newly elected General Zia ul-Haq.

The jubilant General yesterday toasted his victory with his favourite tipple – cold tea and a dash of soda – until an aide pointed out that celebration would appear more tactful after the election.

Said his Highness: "This poll is a rare opportunity for the nation to choose the kind of administration it wants. And that's the way we're going to keep it," he added. "Rare."

Teetotalitarian

His Exalted Sobriety was among the first to cast his vote in a ballot so secret that only he knew where the polling station was. In a gesture which showed his eagerness to sow the seeds of democracy, His Relentlessness voted a few more times and went home for a celebratory nail through the hand. "Aaargh!" he quipped.

Despite the fact that this was a General Election, there were one or two irreligious sons of self-polluting donkeys who refused to vote for the only general standing. But by lunchtime His Flagellance was confidently predicting a landslide. "Just as soon as we get the Opposition to huddle together under a cliff," he added, tenaciously crunching a gravel paratha.

Then it was off to meet the public for His Absolute Ginormity – but sadly, visiting hours were over. And as the sun set slowly over the rascally monkeys of the West, the country's returning officers began the happy task of locating General Zia's voters and returning their children. Such is the bounty of His Incredible Bulletholiness!

Absolute End

For the General, it was the perfect end to a perfect day, as exhausted he threw himself down a stairwell while his entourage applauded his manifest piety. "And there's more to come," foamed His Googliness. "I promise a return to civilian rule in five years' time. That's when I'm leaving the army." Tell us more, general. We're all Zia's!

General Zia illustrates the true meaning of a government of national unity. (From right to even further right) Minister of the Environment and Prisons, Minister of Education and Prisons, Minister of Finance and Prisons, Minister of Agriculture, Fisheries and Prisons, Minister for Extreme Oppressiveness, Minister of Looking like General Zia, Minister of Finding Scapegoats, Minister for Knocking on Their Doors in the Middle of the Night, Minister for Shooting Them.

YOUR TOP TEN PUNISHMENTS
compiled by BARB

	CRIME	PUNISHMENT
1	Blasphemy	Gargling with paint stripper
2	Stealing	Moulinex Manicure
3	Foppishness	Jump leads on the nipples
4	Self-Pollution	Ground glass in the prepuce
5	Drinking Alcohol	Curry paste in the eyes
6	Drinking Coca-Cola	Vindaloo enema
7	Adultery	1 night of passion with Edwina Currie
8	Wearing jeans	Hot cocoa down the Y-Fronts
9	Listening to Western Music	Barbed wire headphones
10	Listening to Lloyd-Webber's Requiem	Listening to Lloyd-Webber's Requiem

GOVT. HEALTH WARNING:
Don't drink and live

IT'S A QUEER WORLD!

Chief Executioner Ali Khan had the surprise of his life when he amputated the hand of convicted shoplifter, Mohammed ul-Wazuq. "When I got the hand home I discovered it was wearing the bracelet that was stolen from my wife over 14 years ago. The ways of Allah are indeed inscrutable!" Well, we've got to "hand" it to you, Ali!

COR-AN!

Phwor! Wouldn't you like to "mecca" Khyber pass at lovely, unwesternised Fatima ul-Foqhs (48-32-36 – but you'll have to take our word for it, lads). And she's not just a pretty face – we believe. Her hobbies include cutting her husband's toenails, mucking out the goat and chopping vegetables, but her ambition is to have a career in business. She won't, of course, 'cos she's a woman!

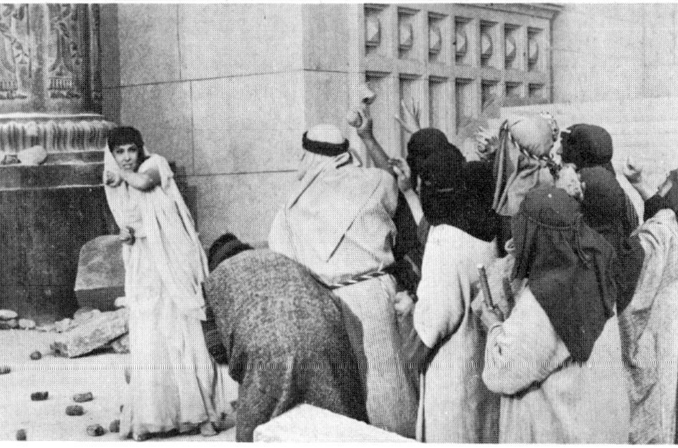

SPOT THE STONE

This week's picture comes from the 3rd round of the Adultery Cup (The State *vs* Mrs Benazir Patel). Last week's winner, Mr Imram Haq of Peshawar, wins a three Rupee water token.

T.V. CHOICE

6.30 No, Minister, No No, Please. Help! Aaargh!
9.30 Last of the Summer Water
9.35 A Bhutto of Barbed Wire

MINISTRY OF DEFENCE
Main Building Whitehall London SW1A 2H
Telephone 01-218 1066 (Direct Dialling)
01-218 9000 (Switchboard)

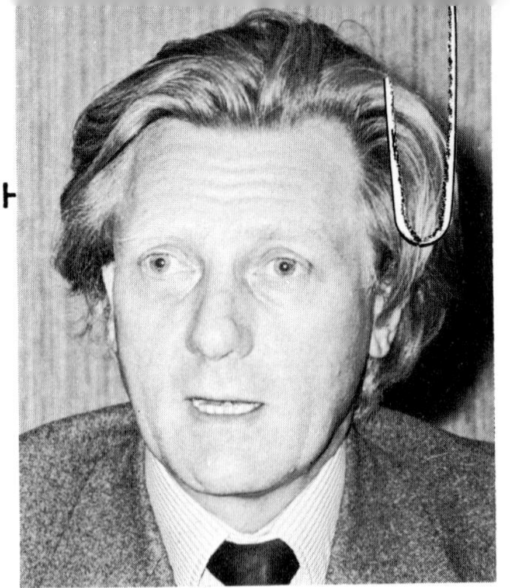

Dear fellow peace-lover,

I am delighted to have been asked to contribute to this book of comedy because it gives me a first-rate opportunity to outline the Government's defence policy.

The SCPM (So-Called Peace Movement) urges one-sided Nuclear Disarmament. Yet they totally fail to take into account that it is thanks to our nuclear deterrent that we have had peace in Europe for 40 years. During the Second World War there was a list of countries as long as my hair which fell under the jackboot of tyranny and not one of them had nuclear weapons. But nowadays, now that they've been invented, well, I hardly think Mr. Hitler dare risk it again.

"But hold on," you say, and you have every right to. "Do we really need all these confusing new missiles, like Cruise and Trident?" Well, of course we do. We must build up our defences so we're able to negotiate from a position of strength. The Russians, on the other hand, are developing their missiles because they want to take over the world. But then, that's just the sort of reason they would have.

Nevertheless, some of these naive flower people from CND tell us nuclear weapons are immoral. Well, I've no time for unilateral morality. We can only be moral if Russia's going to be moral too. In any case, what do we gain from being moral? I'll tell you. The Grand Total of nothing. But we stand to lose all American investment in Britain. That's where morality gets you.

Well, I hope you've managed to follow what I've been saying. I know it's all a bit complicated but have a think and you'll see that those of us who believe in many-sided disarmament, we're the real peace movement. I think our vast nuclear stockpile attests to that. And we're accumulating more peace all the time.

Your friend

Michael Heseltine

pp Winston Churchill

PEACE THROUGH DEATH

Your new home isn't very far away*

**LOOKING FOR A NEW HOME? OF COURSE YOU ARE.
WE'VE JUST BULLDOZED YOUR OLD ONE.**

We at Botha Homes know that everybody wants a pleasant house, fertile land, and easy access to work and shops. But not everybody's white. So the rest of you will have to be shipped off to some jerry built shanty town 60 miles from anywhere.

YOUR BOTHA HOME HAS THE FOLLOWING STUNNING FEATURES:

- Solar heating – when the sun's out, you're warm!
- Split level roof
- Guaranteed cavity insulation (we're still working on the insulation part)
- Instant warm water – there's a crack in the lavatory bowl.
- Each home has an imposing drive–300 miles from civilisation.

B·O·T·H·A

BUILDING HOUSES TO MAKE HOLES IN

You'll be closer than ever to your family – it's 6 to a room.
And you won't miss your friends – we're carting them out too!

*from a hovel

LAW REPORT

Central Criminal Court. The last day of *The Full Weight of the Establishment v. Ponting* before Mr. Justice McCowan. Mr. Amlot prosecuting.

Mr. Justice McCowan: Members of the jury. You have listened most patiently to my summing up. Have you reached a verdict?
Foreman: No. M'lud.
McCowan: Why not?
Foreman: We haven't heard the trial yet.
McCowan: Oh very well. Counsel for the prosecution, you may proceed... and good luck.
(*The defendant was called.*)
Mr. Amlot: Mr. Ponting. I put it to you that you wilfully leaked information originally intended for Mr. Heseltine.
Ponting: That's right.
Amlot: M'lud, I suggest this man knew he could compromise national security by passing it to someone who was totally untrustworthy.
Ponting: Exactly – so I gave it to Mr. Dalyell as well.
McCowan: Then you admit it?
Ponting: Yes, M'lud. The material wasn't classified.
Amlot: Ah -- but there's an awful lot of stuff that is.
Ponting: What!?
Amlot: One thing leads to another, m'lud. First he's feeding titbits to some socialist. Before we know it, he'll be round the Albanian Embassy for beer and sandwiches.
McCowan: Hear, hear.
Ponting: This is ridiculously unfair.
McCowan: Rubbish! We changed the jury when you objected.
Ponting: Only because I recognized the Prime Minister. Anyway, where's my defence counsel?
McCowan: Mr. Ponting. May I remind you that it was on your insistence that we put Mr. Laughland in a position to see the "Crown Jewels"?
Ponting: Yes, but I didn't mean the Tower of London.
McCowan: Silence when you address the court!
Ponting: But this whole trial's just a blatant political exercise – all these questions are irrelevant.
Amlot: Nonsense. Now then, are you or are you not Sarah Tisdall?
Ponting: Of course I'm not.
Amlot: Aha! M'lud this proves the man's a liar... and there I rest my case.
McCowan: Better not – he might nick it. (*Laughter*) Ladies and gentlemen of the jury, you have heard the evidence in defence of Mr. Ponting – but don't let that influence your decision. I certainly wouldn't trust him – his eyes are too close together. Moreover, in the interests of the state and my knighthood, I implore you to consider the careers of several Cabinet ministers, and the plight of their wives, children and mistresses. (*Cries of 'Bravo' from the prosecuting counsel.*)
Amlot: That's the ticket!
McCowan: Now then. Foreman of the Jury. Do you find the defendant guilty, or are you going to make things awkward?
Foreman: Not guilty, m'lud.
Tomorrow: *Mr. Justice McCowan v. The Jury on the Ponting Trial*

Corkhangers Hall. *Royal Commission of Enquiry into British Nuclear Tests in Australia.* Mr. Justice Ocker in the Chair.

Mr. Justice Ocker: I hereby declare the final session of this Enquiry open. Where are we up to?
Counsel: The Australian Tests, My Lord.
Ocker: What's cricket got to do with it?
(*An employee of the British government was called.*)
Ocker: Name?
Witness: I'd rather not say.
Ocker: Very well. Do you swear to tell the truth, the whole truth, and nothing but the truth?
Witness: I'd prefer not to, actually.
Counsel: What?
Witness: Oh, it's all been agreed. Witnesses testifying on behalf of the British Government are not to be prosecuted for perjury if you catch us telling the odd porky.
Counsel: Well answer me this: did the British Government give sufficient warning of the danger attached to being in the vicinity of a nuclear explosion?
Witness: Well, we did tell people that there might be a bit of a bang. And we issued all personnel with special equipment.
(*Counsel examined his brief.*)
Counsel: That would be the "stout pair of sunglasses and an extra ration of athlete's foot powder"?
Witness: We did tell them not to look directly at the explosion itself.
Counsel: That was to protect their eyesight?
Witness: No, no. That was to protect the explosion. It was a military secret, you see.
Counsel: And I understand there was some problem with the wind?
Witness: Yes, unfortunately some fallout got blown onto a small, slightly populated area.
Counsel: What area was that?
Witness: Melbourne.
Counsel: But don't you think that the British Government has been somewhat cavalier, in exposing Australia to this terrible danger?
Witness: Of course. That's why it was such a jolly useful test. Just like the real thing!

If found please return to:-

PERSONAL

Name Rt Hon Neil Kinnock MP, Leader of Opposition

Address c/o House of Commons, Westminster, London SW1, England, Europe, Northern Hemisphere, The World, The Solar System, The Galaxy

Telephone No. Bedwellty 303 and ask

January 1986

20 Monday 7.30am. Be seen catching bus to Lab. HQ. 2.00pm. ~~Meeting with A. Scargill to discuss sacked miners.~~ Rehearsal for Tracey Ullman video

21 Tuesday 10.40am. ~~barber~~ Hair stylist – Marc at Schumi – King's Rd. (Ginger rinse + scrunch-dry) 3.00pm PM's Question Time (Don't forget Strepsils) 4.00pm Apologise to lads.

22 Wednesday Eurythmics album released – check "Our Price". 12.00 – Meet the Press – Stan's Mobile Chippy. 8pm ~~Meeting with A. Scargill to discuss sacked miners.~~ Poison Girls gig – remember to pogo near cameras!

23 Thursday 9.30 am. Discuss Labour's Defence options with Healey, Benn, and Editor of "The Face". 1.00pm "Punch Lunch" – ask Glenys re content of Hattersley's column (THINK GAGS!)

24 Friday 10 am – free. Arrange meeting with some upcoming popular youthspeak figure – (poss. K. Livingstone?) 5.00pm. Meet Paula Yates for "Tube" interview.

25 Saturday 10am Rugby. Be seen having "a jar" with the lads. 6.00pm watch video of "The Tube". 9.00pm. Scout round for really crowded Indian Restaurant and order take-away in loud voice.

26 Sunday AM – Stand in for Glenys at Dhurry and tablemat stall – Camden Lock. 3.00 – watch video of "The Tube" while Glenys is at Alconbury!!!!

January—February 1986

Monday 27 9am. Meeting of Parliamentary Labour Party to discipline Skinner for wearing Terylene trousers. * Book venue for this year's Conference. (Hippodrome? Ace Brixton? Heaven?) 7.00 Wogan. (Don't forget to plug single)

Tuesday 28 11.30. Shake hands with an Asian. 3.00pm PM's Question Time (Try Megezoids) 4.00pm. Apologise to lads and show them video of "The Tube".

Wednesday 29 12–1pm. Work-out with Glenys at Pineapple (Floral Print tracksuit?) 8.30pm Dinner with George and Andrew (Wham!) Trattoria Imperia (Book Strippagram!)

Thursday 30 11am. ~~Meeting with A. Scargill to discuss sacked miners.~~ Go shopping for hair-gel. 4.00 Shake hands with unemployed youngster. 10pm Fly to Liverpool (Virgin Air l.)

Friday 31 9.00 am. Open the Neil Kinnock Roller Disco, Birkenhead. 12.45, Play pool with a lesbian. Free evening – check out Toxteth Alternative Cabaret scene.

Saturday 1 4.00 am. "Saturday Superstore". (Phone-in on BMX Biking) AM – Shopping for shirts with Kaufmann (Paul Smith, Crolla, Gaultier). 7.30 – Guitar lesson with Billy Bragg

Sunday 2 10.30, Covent Garden – busking with Billy Bragg.
3.15pm. Meeting with A. Scargill to discuss sacked miners. (Throat infection perh.?)

To distinguish them from peace protestors, the Ministry of Defence have issued Molesworth residents with special car stickers.

What hot soup our Prof is in, when he goes out for a spin!

Whirr, whirr, click. "Oh what's the use?"
Sinclair Walk-Car's out of juice!

Follow Professor Clive's adventures every week in the "Financial Times"

DEPARTMENT OF HEALTH & SOCIAL

Alexander Fleming House, Elephant & Castle, L

Telephone 01-407 5522

From the Secretary of State for Social Se

Dear Reader,

I've never written a humour book before but here's a joke. Q. What do you call a pensioner with kidney failure? A. A customer. But enough hilarity. I want to tell you of the Government's six-point plan to improve the quality of life in Britain.

1. To eradicate over-crowding in schools - by abolishing state education for the over-16's.

2. To do away with the dole queue - by doing away with the dole.

3. To solve the NHS crisis - by abolishing the NHS.

4. To usher in a Golden Age - by making people pay for their false teeth.

5. To reduce the number of points in our plan.

I've shown it to the P.M. and she says it's awfully good. Hope you think the same. Oh and by the way, if you're at all worried by the worsening heroin epidemic, worry no longer because we've found a way of placing it beyond the reach of the weak and the underprivileged: we're putting it on prescription.

Yours truly,

Norman Fowler

CUT THIS OUT AND GET
£5 OFF YOUR NEXT VISIT
TO THE DOCTOR!

SPOOLS for SCANDAL
A satirickal diversion for four players as was lately presented in Mr. GARRICK'S new Play-House in the Hay-Market after the manner of She Stoops to HMS Conqueror and the recent most popularly received Wild Oaths.
DRAMATIS PERSONAE
Mr. Secretary Brittan – a foppish dunce .... Mr. Richd. GRIFFITHES
Mr. Secretary of War Heseltine – a miles gloriosus .... Mr. Edwd. FOXE
Mrs. Maggieprop – a foolish matron .... Miss Bette DAVIS
Mr. Justice Sir Michael Havers – a pettifogging counsellor ... The Lord OLIVIER
Mr. Clive Ponting
Miss Sarah Tisdall
Mrs. Katie Massiter
3 naughtie servants . . .
Mr. Henry Dean STANTON
Miss Traceworth ULLMAN
Miss Judith DENCHE

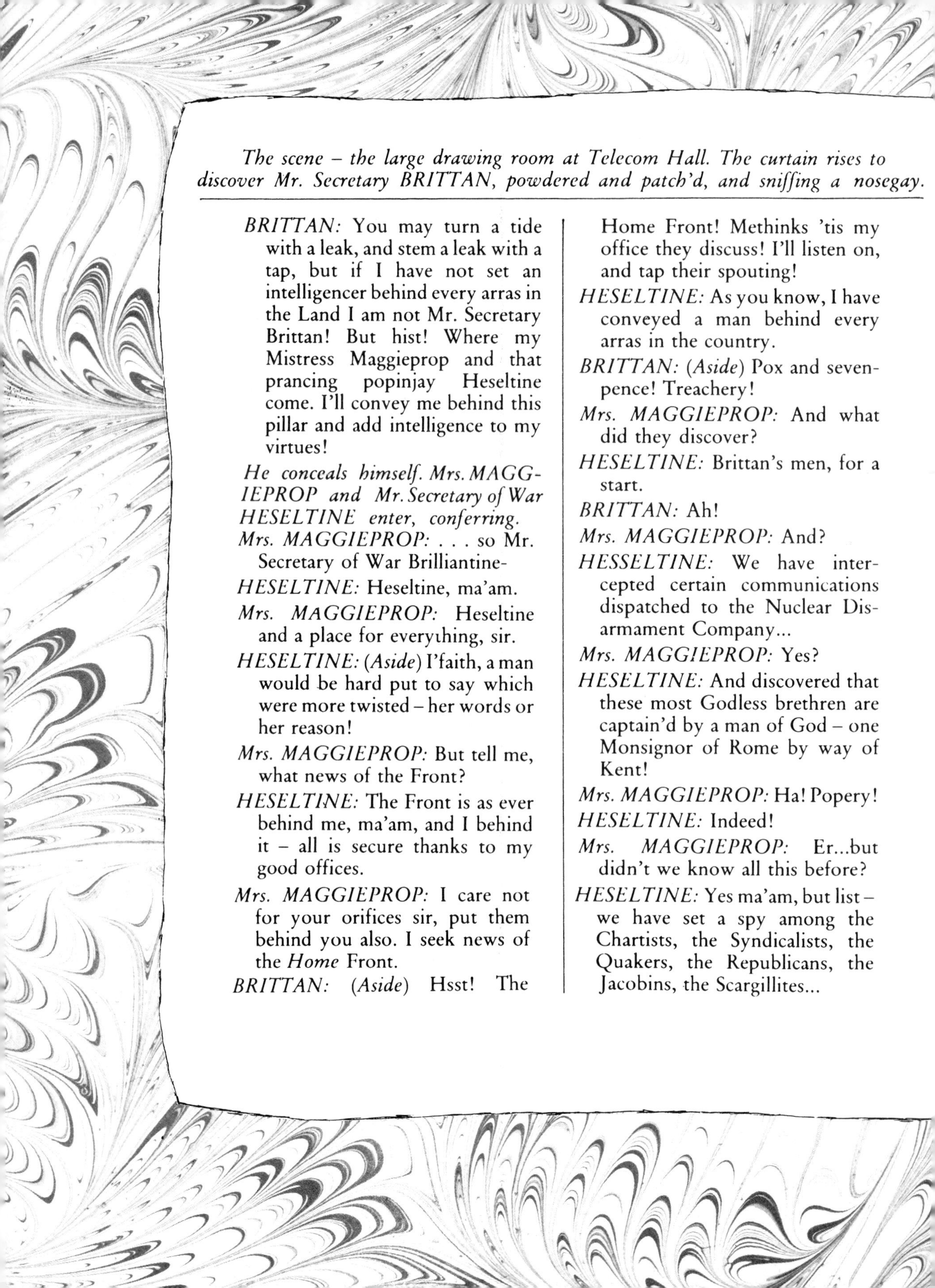

The scene – the large drawing room at Telecom Hall. The curtain rises to discover Mr. Secretary BRITTAN, powdered and patch'd, and sniffing a nosegay.

BRITTAN: You may turn a tide with a leak, and stem a leak with a tap, but if I have not set an intelligencer behind every arras in the Land I am not Mr. Secretary Brittan! But hist! Where my Mistress Maggieprop and that prancing popinjay Heseltine come. I'll convey me behind this pillar and add intelligence to my virtues!

He conceals himself. Mrs. MAGGIEPROP and Mr. Secretary of War HESELTINE enter, conferring.

Mrs. MAGGIEPROP: . . . so Mr. Secretary of War Brilliantine-

HESELTINE: Heseltine, ma'am.

Mrs. MAGGIEPROP: Heseltine and a place for everyihing, sir.

HESELTINE: (*Aside*) I'faith, a man would be hard put to say which were more twisted – her words or her reason!

Mrs. MAGGIEPROP: But tell me, what news of the Front?

HESELTINE: The Front is as ever behind me, ma'am, and I behind it – all is secure thanks to my good offices.

Mrs. MAGGIEPROP: I care not for your orifices sir, put them behind you also. I seek news of the *Home* Front.

BRITTAN: (*Aside*) Hsst! The Home Front! Methinks 'tis my office they discuss! I'll listen on, and tap their spouting!

HESELTINE: As you know, I have conveyed a man behind every arras in the country.

BRITTAN: (*Aside*) Pox and sevenpence! Treachery!

Mrs. MAGGIEPROP: And what did they discover?

HESELTINE: Brittan's men, for a start.

BRITTAN: Ah!

Mrs. MAGGIEPROP: And?

HESSELTINE: We have intercepted certain communications dispatched to the Nuclear Disarmament Company...

Mrs. MAGGIEPROP: Yes?

HESELTINE: And discovered that these most Godless brethren are captain'd by a man of God – one Monsignor of Rome by way of Kent!

Mrs. MAGGIEPROP: Ha! Popery!

HESELTINE: Indeed!

Mrs. MAGGIEPROP: Er...but didn't we know all this before?

HESELTINE: Yes ma'am, but list – we have set a spy among the Chartists, the Syndicalists, the Quakers, the Republicans, the Jacobins, the Scargillites...

Mrs. MAGGIEPROP: Aha! And they are in League with the Tsar!

HESELTINE: Er...not exactly.

Mrs. MAGGIEPROP: It seems, Mr. Heseltine that your pryings are like the fine scabbard you sport there.

HESELTINE: Eh?

Mrs. MAGGIEPROP: Full of cost and empty of point.

BRITTAN: (*Aside*) Ha ha! There my fine redcoat! Soldier fit for a chocolate-house!

HESELTINE: But all I do is Brittan's work.

BRITTAN: (*Aside*) What!

HESELTINE: The man could not spot a mole if the moles were spots on his face. And he has plenty enough of both!

BRITTAN: (*Aside*) He 'marks upon my patches! But I'll patch his remarks yet!

ENTER Sir Michael – greatly agitated.

HAVERS: Oh Calamitie!

Mrs. MAGGIEPROP: But who comes here?

HESELTINE: It is that most Whigg'd of Tories, Mr Justice Havers!

HAVERS: Ahhhh! All our dissembling is expoz'd!

HESELTINE & Mrs. MAGGIEPROP: What! How so!

HAVERS: A certain intelligencer – Mistress Katie Massiter – has turned informer for the gazettes!

EXIT Sir Michael – weeping and rending his garments.

Mrs. MAGGIEPROP: Then this woman must be done!

BRITTAN: (*Discovers himself*) Not so!

Mrs. MAGGIEPROP: (*Surpriz'd*) Bottom!

BRITTAN: Brittan, ma'am.

HESELTINE: (*Aside*) Ha! They say every pillar has its stuffing!

BRITTAN: We cannot do this woman for were she done 'twould prove our undoing. For then all the world will behold our breaches.

Mrs. MAGGIEPROP: Pardon?

BRITTAN: In the Law.

Mrs. MAGGIEPROP: So, in truth 'tis as Master Ponting says: *Quis custodiet ipsos custodes?*

BRITTAN steps forward and addresses the AUDIENCE.

BRITTAN: And gentles – if our play has hurt ye,
Here's a moral to divert ye.
Whatever folly we rehearse,
The play outside is far, far worse.

There follows a PAGEANT of the Siege of FALKLANDS-ISLAND. A Hispanic ARMADA appears captain'd by Don GALTIER. Sir John NOTT in the guise of JOVE is let down by a machine, scattering the fleet with a thunderbolt whereupon the Generall BELGRANE descends beneath the waves. A chear goes up from the assembled company who sing a paean to BRITANNIA, in which guise Mrs. MAGGIEPROP is discovered, brandishing a flaming TRIDENT. The Falklands-Island promptly vanishes. Next, the groves of ALBION are discovered, wherein foregather sundry NYMPHS and SWAINS who are dispers'd by TIPSTAFFS and CONSTABLES in full riot gear. The stage is cleared, and the 3 naughtie servants dance and caper while MERCURY, god of thieves, and messengers convey certain letters to MAD TAM, the OBSERVER gazette, and sundrie personages of the 4th estate and CHANNELL. The 4 PRINCIPALLS step forward to receive their plaudits, but instead are accorded boos and tomatoes by the AUDIENCE, led by Dr Samuel OWEN.

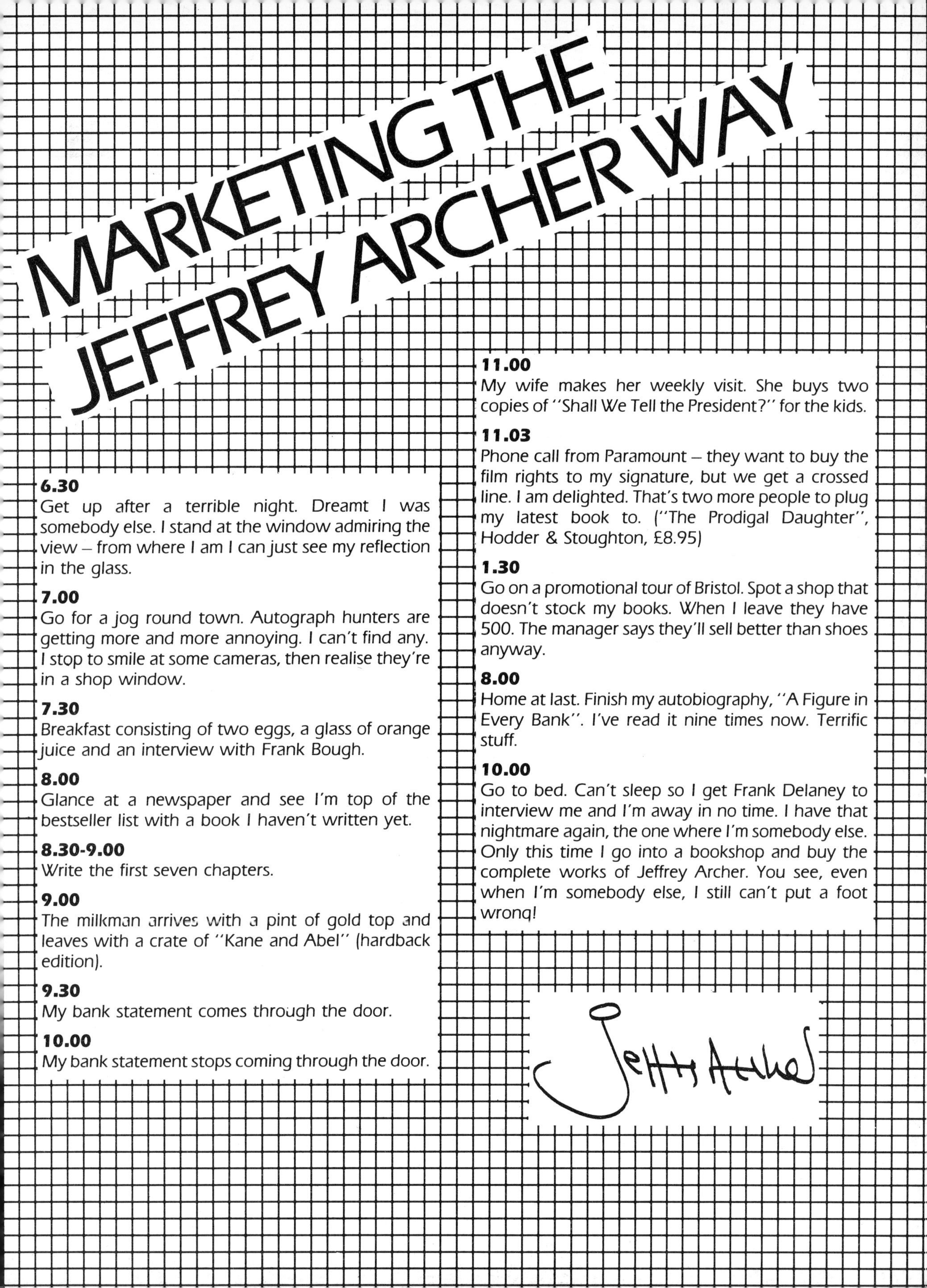

MARKETING THE JEFFREY ARCHER WAY

6.30
Get up after a terrible night. Dreamt I was somebody else. I stand at the window admiring the view – from where I am I can just see my reflection in the glass.

7.00
Go for a jog round town. Autograph hunters are getting more and more annoying. I can't find any. I stop to smile at some cameras, then realise they're in a shop window.

7.30
Breakfast consisting of two eggs, a glass of orange juice and an interview with Frank Bough.

8.00
Glance at a newspaper and see I'm top of the bestseller list with a book I haven't written yet.

8.30-9.00
Write the first seven chapters.

9.00
The milkman arrives with a pint of gold top and leaves with a crate of "Kane and Abel" (hardback edition).

9.30
My bank statement comes through the door.

10.00
My bank statement stops coming through the door.

11.00
My wife makes her weekly visit. She buys two copies of "Shall We Tell the President?" for the kids.

11.03
Phone call from Paramount – they want to buy the film rights to my signature, but we get a crossed line. I am delighted. That's two more people to plug my latest book to. ("The Prodigal Daughter", Hodder & Stoughton, £8.95)

1.30
Go on a promotional tour of Bristol. Spot a shop that doesn't stock my books. When I leave they have 500. The manager says they'll sell better than shoes anyway.

8.00
Home at last. Finish my autobiography, "A Figure in Every Bank". I've read it nine times now. Terrific stuff.

10.00
Go to bed. Can't sleep so I get Frank Delaney to interview me and I'm away in no time. I have that nightmare again, the one where I'm somebody else. Only this time I go into a bookshop and buy the complete works of Jeffrey Archer. You see, even when I'm somebody else, I still can't put a foot wrong!

Jeffrey Archer

A MERGER IS ANNOUNCED

BY MS. A. CHRISTIE

I expect you're all wondering why I've called you into the library,' said Dr Hercule Owen, the world-famous defective. The assembled dignitaries murmured their assent. 'It's because we're having the living room knocked through into the dining room.' He waved his hand vaguely towards another part of his Limehouse stevedore's cottage where two members of socio-economic group 'E' could be heard bringing the East Wing more into line with the Habitat catalogue. His audience tightened their grip slightly on their fork buffet suppers. They were all there: Shirley Williams, the Chief-Defective; Roy Jenkins, the Defective-Inspector; and Bill Rodgers, who was also a defective but they hadn't been able to think of a decent title for him yet.

'It seems, ladies and gentlemen,' continued the doctor, turning to face the window so that they could see his better side, 'that we have a traitor in our midst.'

The others grinned politely, well knowing that Owen's habit of stating the obvious was often the prelude to some startling revelation. Had he tracked down the owner of the mysterious carpet bag bearing the initials 'R.J., Hillhead'? Had he worked out who had stolen the Prime Minister's clothes? Or had he identified the evil saboteur who successfully ground British Rail to a halt every time Shirley Williams had an urgent appointment?

Just then, the library door creaked open and the demi-pair ushered in a slight but commanding figure smartly dressed in a butcher's-stripe kilt.

'Ah, Steel,' intoned the doctor. 'We've been expecting you.'

'Well, that's hardly surprising, is it?' rejoined the Hibernian.

'Ha. You mean my fame as a forecaster is legendary?'

'No, I mean you rang me up yesterday and invited me to-'

'Ha ha ha, well never mind that now.' Owen thrust the other man a bottle of pop and a bag of crisps. 'I have a particular reason for wishing to see you here.' A flicker of dread crossed the Scotsman's face as he realized Owen might be planning yet another photo of the two of them wearing chunky Arran pullovers.

'I have reached the unassailable conclusion, Mr Steel,' Owen flung his other guests a sidelong smirk, 'that you have been plotting a merger.'

Someone gasped. A plate of avocado dip hit the Oxfam hessian carpet.

'That's incredible,' breathed Jenkins. Which was quite a difficult word for him.

'Not at all, Jenkins,' continued the doctor. 'Have you forgotten the deal we made with him?'

'Eh?'

'The *entente cordiale*, 1981?'

'Oh yes. Of course. I think I've still got a couple of cases somewhere.'

'No, no. When we decided that the people were heartily sick of the same old policies that have been ruining the country for the last 25 years.'

'Oh yes, and I suggested an Alliance with the Liberals to hide the fact that most of those policies were ours?'

'Oh forget it, Jenkins.' Owen returned his attention to the diminutive gillie.

'You cannot deny, sir, that following our Alliance's recent electoral successes many of your colleagues have been inciting you to merger?'

'No, I can't deny it.' Steel fingered his sporran nervously. 'But the success was mostly down to the Liberals. There's nothing to suppose I would be driven to such a dastardly course.'

'Ha! But you must also admit that the central policies of our two parties are virtually identical.'

'What do you mean?' skirled the Peeblonian. 'Our defence strategies couldn't be further apart.'

'Really?' A shadow of doubt dimmed the manic gleam in the doctor's eye. 'Then we must have nicked somebody else's.'

'I'm sorry, Doctor,' Steel edged towards the door. 'There's no way I could sell the Liberals out to another party.'

'Aha!' Owen rounded on his prey like a hawk going through the newspapers on TV-am. 'In that case, why do you persist in your claim that the Liberals will lead the next government?'

The colour drained from Steel's knees. Owen returned to the attack.

'Is it not the case, sir, that the Liberals have about as much chance of leading the country by themselves as Cyril Smith has of winning the London Marathon?'

Steel held his peace.

'So your dream of becoming Prime Minister depends on your absorbing one of the other parties in Parliament? A party smaller than your own, but nevertheless commanding a large number of votes? A party whose leader could be used and then quietly done away with?'

'All right, it's true.' Steel broke down utterly – not unlike one of Shirley's trains. 'I knew we were doing well, but we needed something more than a mere electoral arrangement. A solid guarantee of success that would sweep me into Number Ten as the head of a new party.'

'Ha! Well, your little game's up, Steel,' drawled the internationally acclaimed Member for Plymouth, Devonport. 'You thought you could take all the plum jobs for yourself and your chums and fob me off with the Northern Ireland Office. Well it won't work. You can propose merger to me till you're pink in the face. But I'll never agree to it. Do you hear? Never!'

'Who said anything about you?' Steel's brow knitted chunkily. 'I was planning the merger with Kinnock.'

I, CAROL

THE THATCHER SAGA

Chapter One

A new day downs over Dawning Street and it is to-day that I, Carol Thatcher have decided to chronical the life of the Thatcher Dynasty and put it in a book as soon as I have learnt to spell biography. ✓✓ V.G.

sp.

The typing is getting ~~esai easire~~ easier and I am already using two fingers --one to type and the other to scratch my head. Anyway, dear reader, back to incisive reportage. This morning Mumsie (she's the Prime Minister, you know) we know Dadsie and me were having ~~breakfart~~ (If you can still read that, sorry but I can't find the Tippex) breakfast when Daddy said, "Sherrer gm mgg sherrumbat."

Mummy put some more gin on his cornflakes.

"That's better," Dad piped up soberly, "What I said was that I've been chatting to some riporters." sp.

Before Mummy could complete her backswing, he quickly blurted: "It's all right, Margaret, I didn't tell them anything."

Mummy put down the toaster and Daddy continued, "Only that I'm going to South Africa next week to discuss kaffir-quelling tactics in the mines."

Well! The blood drained from Mummy's face quicker than cash from¾ a National Health hospital. Her eyes went all starey like on Panorama as she hissed at Dad across the Wedgewood.

"Denis," she hissed, "You know you're not ment to talk to the press, what with all the trouble our family's been through -- Mark's business deals, Charmaine's bankruptcy and Craig's paternity suit-- (Not really, but I'm trying to spice it up a bit--Carol)-- This'll only make things worse" sp.

As the toaster bounced off Dad's noodle, I piped up consolingly: "Don't worry, Dad. I'll write nice stories about us when I'm a top-ranking ~~jor journel~~ riporter. Look at this article I've written for the Telegraph." sp.

I passed him an article I had written for the Telegraph. Daddy's dark, manly eyes perused the article I had written for the Telegraph and read out the title. Who did? The eye

"What I Done on My Hols by Carol...Hmmm," he said. "I did" or "I have done" not "I done"!

"I wrote it a few years ago, actually," I said.

"Very good, dear," he said.

"Thankyou," I said.

"He said" "I said" Is this all necessary? YES I KNOW BUT I WAS ONLY 18 – C.T.

"But you'd better cross out the bit that says 'C minus minus. Must try harder'" he said.

I, Carol. Chapter One, Page 2

It was only a joke and I certainly wasn't trying to change the subject when I exclaimed, "Mark's late this morning!"

"Three days late," Mother added. "I wonder where he is?"

As if in answer to his question, there was the roar of a powerful engine, a screeching of ~~brakke brakes~~ breaks (No!) and a smashing of flowerpots in the back garden. Mark was coming downstairs. The door flew open and in he came, Mark, my idiot twin brother, though we're really completely different. He's a boy.

"Hiya, folks" he drawled, "Pudding-basin's here! Just popped over to Saudi on the way to the bathroom. Sealed a few contracts, you know."

He plonked himself down at table, spread a few rounds of peanut butter and fish-paste (Yuk!) and poured a cup of tea (mostly on Dad's Sporting Life).

"Mark," said Mumsie mysteriously, "we mustn't be seen together ever again. Do you understand?"

"Oh, come on!" replied her son (Mark) (obvious from context), "Dad doesn't mind."

"No, silly!" replied his mother (Mum) (see above) and she explained how if the Press found out they'd been together, they'll assume they've been doing some business deal. (Too many replied's)

To which Mark replied: "So that's why you're underneath the table. I thought you were keeping Pa company. But Ma," he went on, "did you manage to flog that coffin on your last visit to Moscow--nng!"

Mother had whipped a Liberty's serviette round Mark's scrawny neck--an old trick she'd learnt from the worshippers of the goddess (Good ✓) Kali--(India's "in" at the moment, isn't it? --Carol) and was now setting about stuffing his mouth with a good deal of table cloth. She whispered hoarsely in his ear: "Careful, Mark! Reporters!"

They both looked at me and I slowly put down the phone. And it was then that I vowed never to become ensnaired in this web of greed and ~~corruptio~~ commerce but to describe it in a Bestselling book, "I, Carol", a snip at ~~£7.95~~ £8.95 from Weidenfeld and Nicholson. Then my Mother turned to me and exclaimed:

"Carol! I wish you wouldn't type at the breakfast table."

C minus minus. Must try harder.

Weidenfeld and Nicolson

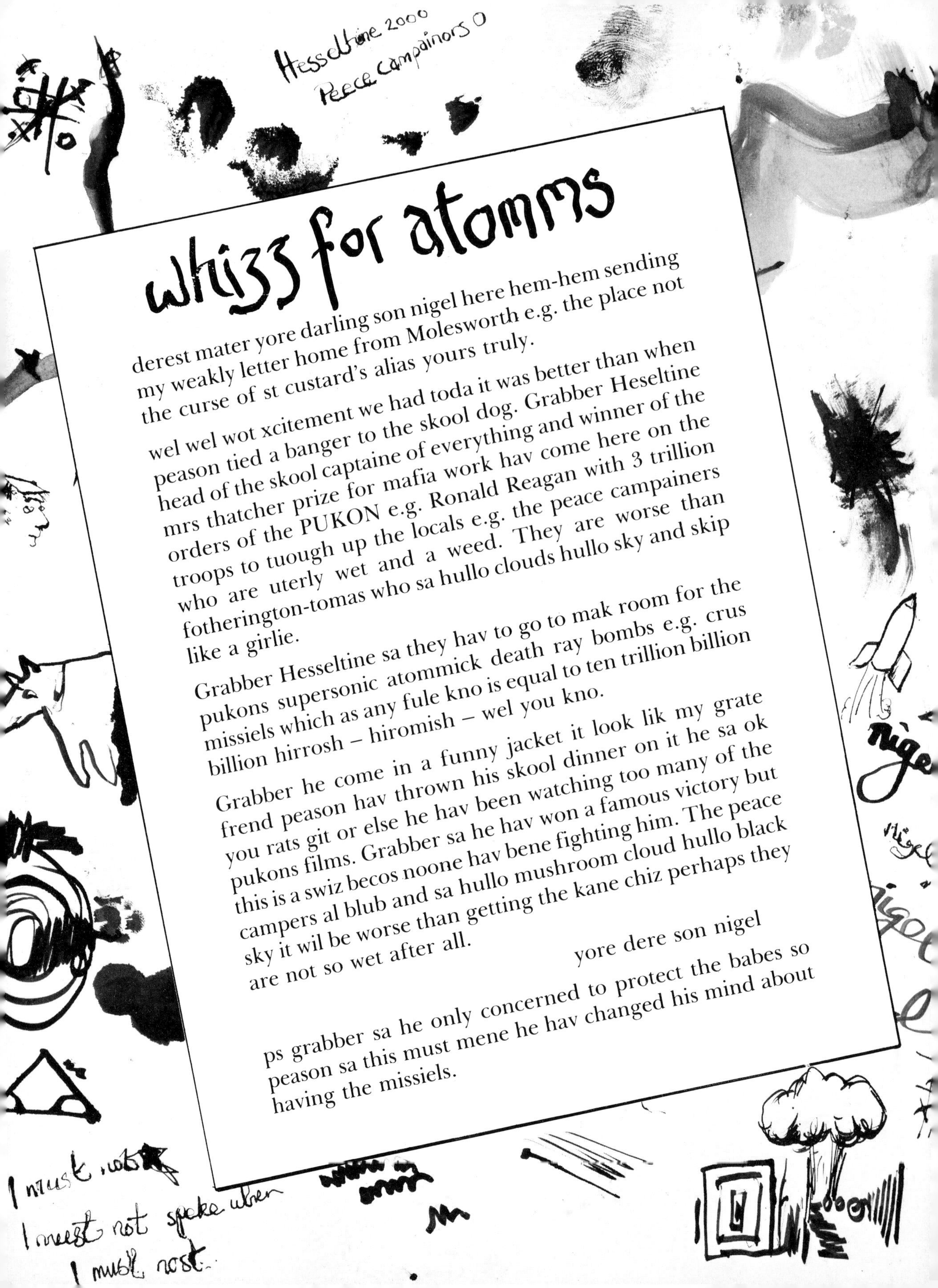

whizz for atomms

derest mater yore darling son nigel here hem-hem sending my weakly letter home from Molesworth e.g. the place not the curse of st custard's alias yours truly.

wel wel wot xcitement we had toda it was better than when peason tied a banger to the skool dog. Grabber Heseltine head of the skool captaine of everything and winner of the mrs thatcher prize for mafia work hav come here on the orders of the PUKON e.g. Ronald Reagan with 3 trillion troops to tuough up the locals e.g. the peace campainers who are uterly wet and a weed. They are worse than fotherington-tomas who sa hullo clouds hullo sky and skip like a girlie.

Grabber Hesseltine sa they hav to go to mak room for the pukons supersonic atommick death ray bombs e.g. crus missiels which as any fule kno is equal to ten trillion billion billion hirrosh – hiromish – wel you kno.

Grabber he come in a funny jacket it look lik my grate frend peason hav thrown his skool dinner on it he sa ok you rats git or else he hav been watching too many of the pukons films. Grabber sa he hav won a famous victory but this is a swiz becos noone hav bene fighting him. The peace campers al blub and sa hullo mushroom cloud hullo black sky it wil be worse than getting the kane chiz perhaps they are not so wet after all.

yore dere son nigel

ps grabber sa he only concerned to protect the babes so peason sa this must mene he hav changed his mind about having the missiels.

PRIVATE JOKE

1/6

No.608,945,231
Nargday
8 Feb '61

(Shome mishtake
shurely? -Ed)

INGRAMS BOMBSHELL!

Ingrome

IT HAS come to my notice that certain members of the public have been claiming that my prestigious organ is merely a collection of old jokes I thought up in 1961.

Let me state categorically that this outrageous slur in no way constitutes the truth and, in fact, they were thought up in 1956 when I was still at Shrewsbury.

These same malcontents are asking – with my organ so much a part of the establishment that it's selling in vast quantities in that august and blameless newsmerchant, W.H. Smith (formerly W.H. Smug) – if it isn't time I stopped printing it on lavatory paper.

And finally, these whingeing sodomites are putting it about that it is somewhat hypocritical that the receiver of so many writs should run whining and blubbing to his lawyers at the slightest whiff of offence to himself.

The matter is now in the hands of my solicitors, Messrs. Fifty, Litigious and Bitter.

I. Hislobes
pp Lord Ingrome
The Goldsmith Suite,
Hotel Adler,
Barbados.

Halley's comet shock appearance – World reels.

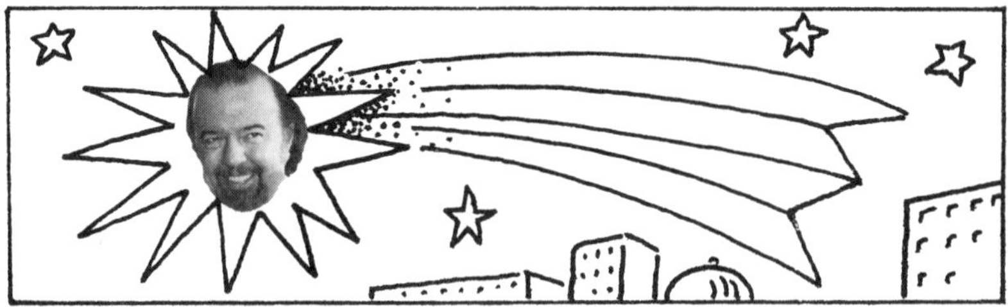

by Lunchtime O'ld Joke

Londoners cowered in terror today as a large body appeared in the sky over the South Bank. Teenagers and pensioners alike wept openly with the shock appearance of the object – later revealed to be the West End impresario Sir Peter Halley, 93, which has not been seen in the vicinity for over 76 years.

Tragi-Comet

TV star gazer Sir Patrick Rees-Moore, 62, explained: "There is no cause for alarm. Sir Peter is mostly composed of gas and the so-called tail is in fact a train of unemployed actors looking for work." He continued: "In olden times the appearance of this sort of thing was taken as an omen of doom presaging terrible events such as 'The Romans in Britain'. But in fact, what's happening is that *Private Joke* have taken two unconnected news stories and slung them together in the hope that it'll be funny." (Shurely shome mishtake – Ed.)

Theatre of Comety

Neasden reeled as Rita Chevrolet, 23, er, er, Brigadier Buffy Cohen (*sic*) er running out of jokes (cont. p.94) Someone nothing to do with this article is 127

NW11 by "HAMPSTEAD"

Drivel

● *Terrible news reaches me today of "Bunter" Wokingham, group editor of a small publishing firm that nobody's ever heard of unless they've been reading "Drivel" every fortnight for the last five years.*

Colourful bachelor Wokingham, 35, has been passed over for the post of managing director in favour of old Etonian fan of Iraqi glass-blowing "Nobber" Lawrence, 42, (see Drivel passim*). So stung was "Bunter" by his lack of preferment that he's leaked details of his rival's extra-marital affairs to* Private Joke.

OLD ETONIAN water sports enthusiast "Nobber" Lawrence, 47, has been up to his old tricks again (see Drivel *passim*). At a party held to celebrate the promotion of ageing Lothario "Donald Duck" Parfitt, 55, Head of the BBC's Paper Clip Procurement Division, "Nobber" was caught "driving up the Chichester by-pass" with Penny Chapman, 33, flame-haired Business Editor of "Small Marketing Consultant's Weekly" (see "Drivel" *passim*).

● *MORE strange goings-on reach my ears from the Aegean paradise of Laxos, tiny Greek hideaway of tiny Greek shipping magnate Spiros Kalamares, 89.*

Recent visitors to the oily foreigner's exclusive retreat include flamboyant publisher "Bunter" (see "Drivel" passim*) and BBC paper clip supremo "Donald Duck", both well-known devotees of "Pyrenean wind-surfing".*

So dreary have the "Squid's" excesses become for his neighbours – including French insurance magnate "Kermit" Lachaise – that a multi-million pound law suit is being brought against Private Joke.

Bernardette is said to be furious, but nobody cares because nobody knows who she is.

THE pastoral idyll of "Chutneys", Sir Rupert Tilehurst's Sussex retreat, was rudely shattered last weekend, if my imagination serves me correctly, when "Bunter" arrived to claim his long-standing Zambian scuba-diving partner "Biggles" Chapman, 32, fictitious husband of raven-haired Penny Chapman, 28, Business Editor of "Small Marketing Consultant's Weekly", from the clutches of the Home Counties' most disgusting MP, 62.

No sooner had "Biggles" fled weeping into the bathroom than a Range Rover bearing "Kermit", "Nobber", "Donald Duck" and the "Squid" knocked over a bollard in Kensington.

Disgraceful scenes ensued, during which a well-known gossip columnist, 43, was heard to remark: "You try keeping the readers interested in the tedious affairs of the same five upper to middle class media people when all you get to put in this column is what they tell you themselves." (See "Drivel" *passim*.)

Plop Plop!

The features below have been held over because the submissions received from readers were too funny.

Colemanballs

£5 paid for contributions

All looney feminist nonsense gratefully received. £5 paid for entries printed.

True Stories

INFORMATION:

I-SPY

£10 paid for similar submissions. *(SAE required for return of photographs. No transparencies.)*

£5 paid for entries

Great Bores Of Today

"...I really don't know what I'd do without it I mean it's kept me in pocket for more years than I care to mention Bailie Vass is 197 you know people wonder how I stay in business what with all these libels we keep printing flame-haired Spiggy Topes, 49, whacking his donger in the kedgeree and *I* say without these libels who'd buy the magazine I think we should be told paranormal waves (see *Joke passim*) of a Ugandan nature Harold Wislon (sic) is 485 that's enough boredom Ed cont'd p. 94...."

Letters

Pathetic Old Bore

Sir,
I would like to point out that the information printed about me in Joke *No. 608, 945, 230 is completely untrue and without foundation. Hope it doesn't happen again!*

Yours,
REV. C.G. PAGETT
The Manse,
Ashton-under-Lyne

Sentimental poove

Sir,
I don't mind being accused of bestiality with a syphilitic giraffe (Joke *No. 608, 945, 227 – 30) but surely my philosophy tutor, as a man of eighty-three recovering from a stroke, deserves sympathy rather than ridicule?*

Yours faithfully,
NIGEL MARTIN
Lincoln College,
Oxford

Stupid ingratiating twat from Bristol

Sir,
Please accept the enclosed cheque for £14 for a year's subscription to Private Joke. *I've enjoyed it for many years. More power to your organ!*

Yours,
DAVID FISHER,
Bristol

Terry Waite – An Apology

In *Private Joke* No. 608,945,216 we suggested that the true purpose of Mr Terry Waite's mission to Libya at the beginning of this year was to give his body to Colonel Gaddafi in return for Cementation Ltd being given the contract to build Libya's fifty-first National Death Camp. We genuinely believed this to be true at the time. And so did the man in the off-licence who told us about it.

We now acknowledge this story to be totally false by printing this in microscopic type at the bottom of the page. But there's no smoke without fire.

POETRY CORNER

In Memoriam:

E.J. Thribb (17)

So. Farewell then
E.J. Thribb.

It was funny
The first few times.

On second thoughts,
No, it wasn't.

E.J. Thribb (17)

HOME OFFICE

Queen Anne's Gate London SW1H 9AT

Direct line 01-213 1984

Switchboard 01-213 3000

Dear Inmate,

A lot of people ... all right stop heckling! I will not be intimidated! ... oh ... er ... you can't heckle, can you? er ... it's a letter isn't it. Ha ha. Um ... a lot of people seem to think of the Home Secretary as someone who heartlessly breaks up immigrant families and wastes the country's resources spying on Guardian readers. But I do other things as well, you know.

For instance, the recent miners' strike showed us some of the worst incidents of violence this country has ever seen. So next time we have a confrontation of this sort I've given strict instructions to the police not to let anyone watch what they're doing. And the problem of soccer hooliganism is now so serious that I've personally intervened and asked the Prime Minister to do something about it.

But there are plenty of other positive aspects to my work - like race relations. How many other Home Secretaries can say they've gone round Bradford in a sari? Then there's prison overcrowding which under my stewardship, I am happy to say, has reached an all-time high. And no-one is more concerned about the erosion of civil liberties than I, but if we're to crack down on the rising tide of violent crime, we must photograph everyone who shops at Habitat. So let me make this quite clear. This government has no place for thugs and bullies. At least not outside the Cabinet.

Yours sincerely,

Leon Brittan

"A Round with Allah"

Well, it's a fine day here at the Royal and Ancient Gulf Course, where there have been so many memorable knockout tournaments over the years. The sun is out and Allah is where he belongs, on my side. After a few practice strokes (40 lashes on some blackguard caught harbouring Iraqi bullets in his chest), we're ready to tee off.

It's the solitude that attracts me to this game – there's just me and the elements and a quarter of a million blood-crazed Iranians.

Saddam and Gomorrah

Suddenly a mist rolls in from the West and it looks like my satanic opponent Saddam is using nerve gas again. Just to make sure I send in 30,000 of my crack sniffer troops. Hmm. Seems I was right. But then I always am and I've got a big man with a scimitar to prove it.

There are some pretty tricky holes on this course – the one I'm aiming for is 300 miles away and is known locally as Baghdad. There's also a couple of sand-traps and a water hazard called the Straits of Hormuz where many a squaddie has lost a ball. I ask my faithful caddy for a club – it's all we've got left now we've run out of Kalishnikovs. That's the problem with this course – supplies. I used to be a dab hand at pitch and run but now hand grenades are harder to come by than a MacDonalds in Teheran.

By now the green is in view: they must have switched to Mustard gas. Time for

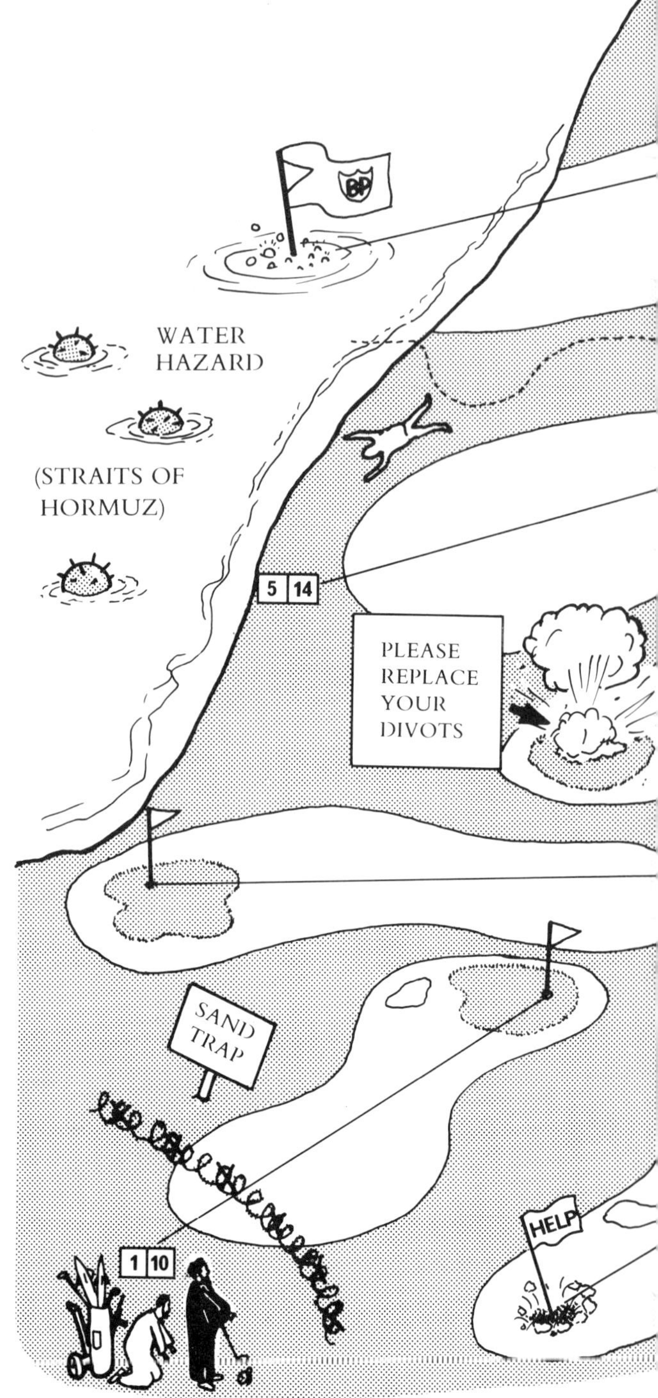

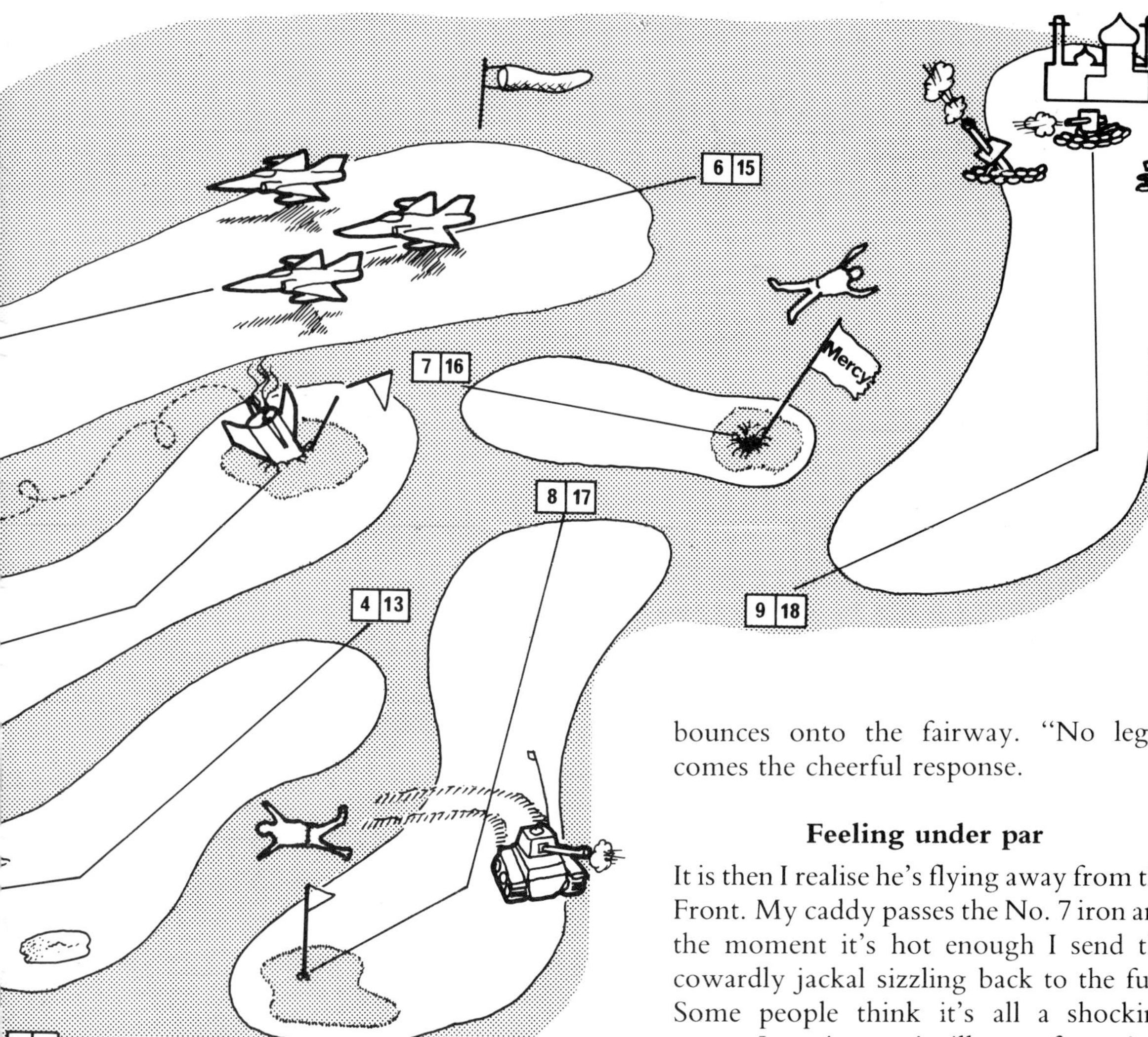

some positive Gulf tactics, I think, and turning once again to my caddy I ask for another club. He says there's no need as we've a fresh delivery of SAM ground-launched missiles. Good old caddy! (It's short for Gadaffi.)

I take a shot. It describes a perfect parabola against the empyrean blue and lands in a bunker. What rotten luck – it's one of ours. This brings a fellow player out to meet us. "What's your handicap?" we ask as he flies past at eye-level and bounces onto the fairway. "No legs" comes the cheerful response.

Feeling under par

It is then I realise he's flying away from the Front. My caddy passes the No. 7 iron and the moment it's hot enough I send the cowardly jackal sizzling back to the fun. Some people think it's all a shocking waste; I say just wait till one of us wins.

And as Allah slowly dims his reading light, we make our devout way to the Royal and Ancient Gulf Clubhouse. I see the Iraqis are already sinking a few oil tankers, mainly.

Well, I knew, sooner or later you've got to bury your differences. At the moment our difference stands at half a million men. That's what I like about life on the Gulf course – it's cheap.

NEXT WEEK: Test Match Special: Ayatollah Khomeini v. the Rest of the World.

ROAD TESTING

Last year the Royal Family cost the public three billion billion pounds. But are we getting value for money? We tested a sample of regal personages – from the top, bottom and middle price range. This was a welcome opportunity to see how they measured up as the last time we attempted this was in 1982. On that occasion our tests had to be cut short when one of our researchers was discovered in the Queen's bedroom with half a bottle of wine.
The trials consisted of:

- opening a factory
- touring an old people's home
- attending the independence celebrations of a developing African state.

Models scored bonus points for being Colonel-in-Chief of an Army Regiment, showing potential for a sense of humour and getting into Oxbridge with a CSE in Pottery.

Her Majesty the Queen

ZZZZZZZZZZZZ
(especially at Christmas)

Clothes: Hylda Baker's hand-me-downs

A good all-round performer, but we could have wished for a bit more variety in the factory tour. Though endearing to start with, the relentless beaming and the repeated enquiry: 'And how long have you worked here?' began to pall. The voice is unfortunate, but we put it down to a design fault.

The Queen has an excellent sense of humour, and rounded off her speech to the President and people of Ikebeland by telling the Mark Phillips joke. Ten out of ten for delivery there, but unfortunately they'd already heard it.

The visit to the old people's home went well; however, a footman had to return the next day with several hearing aids, catheters and sample jars which she had mistaken for presents.

HRH Prince Edward

ZZZZZ

Clothes: Hacking jackets; Cloth caps; Rugby boots.

While at University this model has displayed astonishing intellectual skills – mostly those of his bodyguard, Detective-Inspector Dobson (D. Phil., Oxon). His inability to tell a joke in no way impaired his capacity for making our panel of journalists laugh, and his tour of Ikebeland was so successful that it has now transferred to the West End. Sadly, Edward offended the factory workers by doing his Footlights cockney accent, but was extremely popular at the old people's home. We found out later that they thought he was Henry Kelly.

HRH Prince Charles

ZZZ

Clothes: Savile Row tailored wetsuit.

Fairly difficult to restrain, this one, according to his handler, Princess D****, since he is always dashing off to strange and exotic places, like Bali, Australia, Sri Lanka, and the Raymond Revuebar. He tells a passable version of the Mark Phillips joke, marred only by the bad Neddy Seagoon impression. There was a moment's confusion in Ikebeland when he thought he was touring a Toxteth youth club, and again at the factory, where presumably influenced by his Uncle Dickie, he attempted to form a strike committee. Finally, at Twilight Towers Home for Old Folk, Charles had enormous success at dealing with hecklers, owing to the fact that their teeth had been confiscated.

Key to Symbols

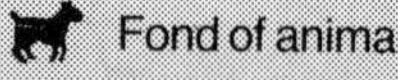
Fond of animals

Very fond of animals

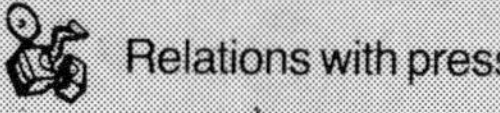
Relations with press

Baldness quotient

Past girlfriends

Z Public speaking

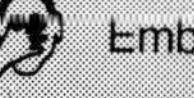
Embarrassing husband

THE ROYALS

Her Majesty visits Smithfield to choose a new chimney sweep.

Edward nearly fails the factory tour test by turning up in the wrong clothes.

Learning to walk – Charles picks up a few tips.

Anne opens the Whiskas factory by riding the ingredients into the grinder.

Prince Philip grouse-shooting at Balmoral.

Andrew opens a gay disco in Huddersfield.

HRH Princess Anne

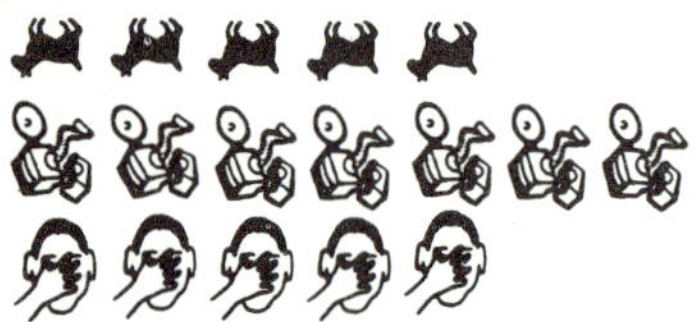

Clothes: Headscarves; Hunting pinks; Jackboots.

What a performer! At the factory she really hit the mark! But he promised not to speak to any more photographers. At the old people's home she made quite an impact though the front wall has now been rebuilt. She has come in for a lot of unfair criticism for alleged rudeness and arrogance but her behaviour at the African independence celebrations was impeccable. It was even more of a disappointment, then, when she faltered at the last moment by staging a military coup, imprisoning the President and banning political meetings. She is married to the Mark Phillips joke.

HRH Prince Andrew

Clothes: The Roger Moore look; Swimming trunks (worn on head)

A former chopper pilot, this make of Royal is always boasting about the size of his helicopter. The factory visit was deemed a great success, and he found a lot in common with several of the female packers. But sadly, the supervisor was forced to intervene with a bucket of cold water. Apparently Andrew thought this a terrific jape and rampaged round Quality Control setting off the fire extinguishers.

In Ikebeland he used the Mark Phillips joke and beefed up the punchline by pushing the President into a river. The residents of Twilight Towers were a little tired by now and pelted the Prince with rice pudding and bits of broken furniture. However, the day ended with a minor triumph when Andrew swapped phone numbers with Mrs Doris Waverly, 84.

HRH Prince Philip, Duke of Edinburgh

ZZZZZZZZZZZZ

Clothes: Any military uniform, except those without a hat.

Imported from the Continent, this Greek model is rather rough around the edges. His rendering of the Mark Phillips joke was competent but included some rather scatological embellishments. The factory visit was fair, but Philip slipped up badly when he asked the Prime Minister how long she had worked there. Luckily everyone thought it was a joke. And a diplomatic incident was narrowly avoided when he lectured the Cabinet of Ikebeland on birth control, but everyone thought that was a joke too.

His position as President of the World Wildlife Fund brings him into contact with animals at close quarters, which is a boon because his aim is not as good as it used to be. As for his relations with the press, Philip once told a brace of photographers to get off his land, and they had to emigrate. Twilight Towers had been closed down.

Civil List	Uncivil List
The Queen	Prince Philip
Princess Anne	
Prince Edward	
Prince Charles	
Prince Andrew	

Conclusions

The Royal Family varies in price and quality, so there's something here to suit every price and pocket.

The Queen Comfortable, roomy estate (4,000,000,000,000,000 acres approx). Comes with spare tyre.

Prince Philip Ex-fleet Ford Consort. Only one owner (old lady who uses it on Sundays).

Princess Anne Popular touring model with swift gear change. Specially strengthened rear.

Prince Edward Low-powered, lightweight. The Royal Family's answer to the Sinclair C-5.

Prince Andrew Low, fast sports model with plenty of poke. Handles smoothly and is quick to get out of skids, though lady users may find too much play in the clutch.

Prince Charles Sometimes known as the Mini Clubman, he's only recently gone into production. Several models have been tested but in the end he married Lady Diana Spencer.

However, in our view, the make we'd go for is the one we consider the most intelligent, polite, cheap and articulate – HRH Prince Harry.

The Wit of Prince Charles

Why is the Prince of Wales considered the wittiest of the Royals?

Here are a few of his side-splitters.

'Hello, Neddy.'

'He's fallen in the water!'

'That's something I've always wanted a crack at.' (To a septic tank cleaner.)

'Kangaroo meat and lager mostly.'

'I must get one for my wife.'

'Why was that?'

1

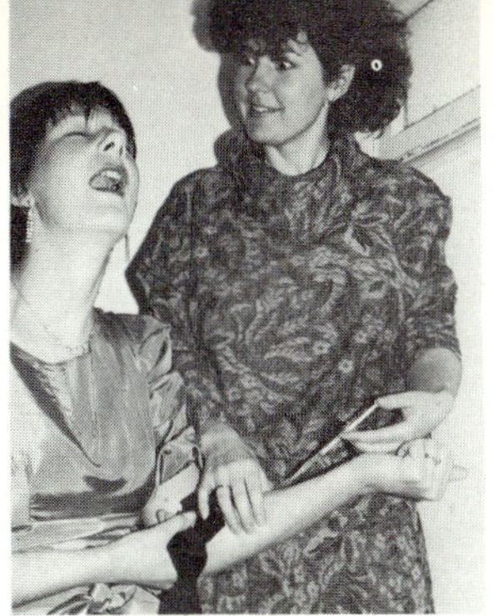

2

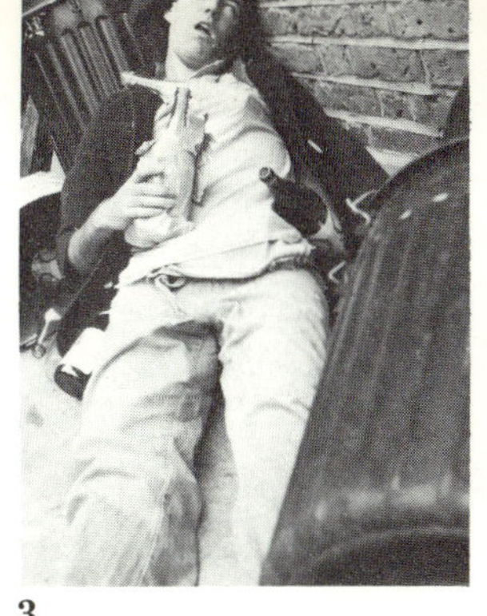

3

4

1 The Hon. Jeremy Rimmington-Spencer plays one of the games at the **Annual Charity Gala, Kensington**: Blow Football. **2 The Deb of the Year Contest:** Lady Charlotte Fortescue-Brown and Belinda Stuart Mastiff share a joke. **3** Giles Gooch-Jeffries soaks up the atmosphere at **Glyndebourne.** Too many strawberries! **4** The morning after, **Berkeley Square**. Alistair Maypole-Heath, Belinda Stuart Mastiff, Flicky Bulstrode-Stirrup and Jeremy Maypole-Heath.

Jennifer's Diary

This week, as in any other, I've been seeing what a fine example our bright young townsfolk set to the rest of the country. The first date in my diary was the Annual Charity Gala at the Peddlers' Hall, Kensington. This was a marvellous bash got up by these youngsters in aid of Columbian Agriculture. I asked the Hon. Gordon Pryce Ogilvy Stevens if the white substance being passed round on mirrors was South American Self-Raising Flour. He replied laughingly, "You could say that." I then told him that his work was certainly not to be sneezed at. He laughed again, and I commented how nice the weather had kept. He laughed yet again. Such an amiable young man! He was still laughing when I left. Happy days!

On to the Deb of the Year Contest where I noticed how many young ladies are training to be nurses or, at least, so I presume from the number of syringes on show. Thence to Glyndebourne where I met young Jeremy Maypole-Heath who seems to be taking a large number of blue hay-fever tablets, poor dear! He explains he doesn't want to come down just yet and I wholeheartedly agree. Make the most of Oxford while you can!

After a most enjoyable opera, Rossini's *Il Mercatore delle Droge*, it's back to London for the Berkeley Square Ball. There I asked the very eligible Charles Everett Posner to pass the canapés but he must have misheard because instead I received a rather aromatic white cigar. Hee hee. Whoops! I feel a bit giddy. Let's have a love-in!

I, Carol

THE THATCHER SAGA

Chapter Thirty-Five

Must you start every chapter like this?

A new day dawns over Downing Street and it is to-day that I, Carol Thatcher, cast my mind back to ~~my idiot twin brother's~~ Mark's big weekend. (Or two big weekends as it turned out!) The weekend when Mummy, the Prime Minister, was to meet beautiful Texan heiress, Karen or Diana Something-or-other (FIND OUT), Mark's true lover, or "meal ticket" as he put it, rather prozaicly (Sp), I thought.

The weekend at Chequers went swimmingly at first (you know, tea and shortbread, deck-~~quotes~~-quoits and only a couple of embarrassing Dad-related incidents). But then on Sunday, Mummy announced that we all had to attend this service in the local church. We were all a bit surprised because we usually only go when somebody's died or there's been a big war or something, but Mummy said later something about showing off the rich girl while we've got her.

Anyway, dear reader, Mummy, ~~Diane~~ Karen and I, Carol, travelled in the Daimler, while Daddy and Mark followed in the Porshe (Sp).

"Don't let Mark drive," came Mum's tearse (Sp) warning before we set off, but to no avail: Dad had hit the Bristol Cream hard that day, so, as Mark explained afterwards, there really was no alternative. That earned him a severe tongue-lashing from Mum, I can tell you! (There's nothing she likes worse than people pinching her ~~quoits~~ quotes.)

Anyway, suffisit to say, they got lost. (Well, you saw it coming, didn't you, readers?) And Mummy, ~~Karen~~ Diane and I, ~~Carol,~~ (stop it!) had no alternative (!) but to go into the church alone.

It was a quiet service: just family, friends and one hundred photographers. I was deeply moved by the religiousness of the occasion, During one of the hymns I didn't know the tune of, I ~~sup supply~~ supplely got Karen's attention.

"Psst!" I went supplely. → I think the word you are striving for is "subtly".

Mark's equally dim girlfriend took ages to notice that I wanted a chat and carried on pretending to know the tune.

"Pssssst! Karen! That's a whopping great ring you're wearing!"

"Thank you," she replied, "It's from Mark."

Well! This was grist for the gossip columns! My insicive riporter's (sp) mind wanted to know more. "Does this mean that Mark--?"

"Sold it to me. Yes."

I put his IQ up a couple of notches as I groped my way through the last verse. The ~~hymen~~ (Ooops, don't read that. I think it's the rudest mistake I've made yet! Ever!)

The hymn finished and we filed out. Karen was discretely guided towards the photo- X
plural not genitive!!
grapher's by the gentle prodding of Mummy's electrode. But Mark and ˘ad were nowhere to be seen, let alone photographed.

again!
X Anyway, sufisit to say, they finally turned up for the buffet lunch at Chequers the next weekend, with Dad cradling a bottle of Tibetan table wine and Mark asking whether you get igloos in Buckhinghamshire, of all things! X Sp

But what a glorious event it was! All the family friends were there: the Director of Cementation, the Chairman of Scott Lithgow, the Imperial High Wizard of Trafalgar House. After lavish dessert of tangerine jelly and piped Dream Topping, Mark, ~~Karen~~ Diane and I ended up in the Bonar Law Suite. Almost immediately I sensed that the two lovebirds wanted to be alone. This was ~~there~~ their time, ~~they're~~ their brief moment of intimacy, so I left them on the sofa and hid behind the curtain.

The young Texan beauty immediately slid along the sofa towards Mark at about 100mph. "So we're alone at last," she murmured. (That's what she thought!) "Kiss me! Kiss me!"

"What, twice?" said Mark curling his lip ever such a little.

* "I want to feel your mouth on my neck, you big stallion." * Good!

"Oh, all right," Mark breathed passionately, "but first tell me how much your old man's got in the bank."

"Ten million dollars." X

"O.K. Here goes!" and so crying he gave her a burning peck on the nape.

"Mark, Mark, oh, Mark." she groaned, "you've left ~~you're~~ your chewing gum behind."(Typical!) When he had untangled the small sticky blob from her raven tresses and put it safely back in his mouth, he appeared at a loss for words. "Um, look, er, Kare-, Di-, er, Tittipoos, we've had a marvellous time these past few days. Um, you know, sort of."

Do we need this?
WELL IT HAPPENED C.T.

"Go on, my love." Her voice was warm and encouraging ~~and only a little upset about the chewing gum business~~.

"Well, there's something I must ask you."

"Yes?" she quavered, hardly daring to guess Mark's next words.

"Could you foot the bill for the airfare home?"

Across her exquisite features (actually, she's nothing special) came an expression I could not quite fathom, mainly because one of Mum's big rubber plants was in the way. She stood up and moved towards the door, as if to close it on clan Thatcher FOREVER. But Mark, dear twittish Mark, called her back. "Hey, Botpot!" he cried, "Can you hear typing?"

X "Uh-oh," I thought and vowed never to become a ~~mere~~ ~~mear~~ mere scribbler of salacious eavesdroppings but to pen such deep and inciteful works such as "I, Carol" a snip at ~~£8.95~~ 99p from Mills and Boon.

THE END (It's not very good, is it?)

Don't worry, dear. We'll get somebody to ghost it.
Mills and Boon

WE'VE GOT

As you may have heard, we in the DHSS have begun to issue new, handy and durable plastic National Insurance Numbercards to replace those nasty old stupid cardboard ones that were such an awful nuisance.

Nightmare

This is simply because we want to make things easier for you, the suspect, to fit into the new computerised National Insurance records. Now, some people have been saying that these cards are thinly disguised National Identity cards and that it's part of some "Orwellian Nightmare". Yes, some people have been saying this, but thanks to the cards, we know *exactly* who they are and what to do with them.
How does the new card work?

NATIONAL INSURANCE NUMBER CARD

NI Number
AQ 1298 2QXTROTSUBV. RM101

WINSTON SMITH

WARNING! THIS STRIP FOR POLICE USE ONLY

Criminal

Well, we just pop it into a computer, and hey presto! The name and National Insurance number come up on a screen. No mention at all is made of the holder's criminal record, or the fact that he's late with his hire purchase payments on the car, or his wife's affair with the doctor. Now, who will get these new cards?

Desperate

Well, eventually everyone, but initially school leavers, people on the dole, immigrants, working mothers – in other words, cases of desperate need, cases where we desperately need to have the information. So as you can see, it's all for *your* benefit. Because if you don't use the cards, you won't get the benefit.

Invasion

But if you're still concerned about invasion of privacy and civil liberties – don't worry – apply to:

The Strange Looking Water Board Van,
Parked for the Last Week,
Outside-Your-Front-Door,
CL1 4AE

Issued by the Department of Health and Social Security.

YOUR NUMBER

NORMAN'S WISDOM

Ha ha! Hello there! Norman Willis here – that's right, your old Uncle Norman with another precious nugget of Norman's Wisdom. Now, I'm a chap who's given a lifetime's service to defending the rights of ordinary working people, but these days I'm General Secretary of the TUC, so I have to be a bit careful what I say! Still, I'm in a unique position to see things from all points of view – from the right wing of the Tory Party all the way to the right wing of the Labour Party. So I like to poke my head round the door from time to time to let you know Norman's on your side – whatever side that happens to be.

Now, some of you workers out there probably like going on strike from time to time. Nothing wrong with that. But you can't beat the old way of thrashing out your differences by reasoned argument and peaceful persuasion. Then when you've done that you're ready to go and negotiate with management. All right. I know there are some folk who are dead against getting round the table with the bosses. But for me, there are three main advantages. (1) You get a cup of tea. (2) There's no unpleasantness (unless you're sharing a blotter with Arthur Scargill – ha ha! – just joshing Arthur!). (3) There's every chance that you'll get biscuits as well – Gypsy Creams too, not those boring ones with the names of French seaside resorts scratched on the top. But I digress. The thing is, if you're prepared to be sensible and see the other chap's point of view, you may not get everything your members demand, but you will get a peerage, eh Frank? Ha ha!

Now, a word about Militants. (My Auntie Bea says she can remember when a Militant was somebody who sold hats! Ha! Ha! You can see where I get it from!) Now, it's clear to me that we've got to root out the extremists from our movement – it's the only way I'll get Hammond to stop nagging me to do something about it. But you've got to be even-handed. So I propose to deal with them in exactly the same way as I sorted out the EETPU and the AUEW when they broke TUC rules and accepted government money for secret ballots. There was no time for procrastination or mealy-mouthed resolutions. The situation called for strong, positive action. So I set up a committee to look into the whole business.

Anyway, that's about it. But if ever you get into a pickle just drop us a line and we'll give you every last ounce of support the TUC has it in its power to muster. I'm sorry, but it's all we've got. Cheerio!

Norman Willis

PS: Now that the coal dispute's over we can all go back to supporting the miners. Dig Deep!

PPS: A little secret I discovered on my visit to Number Ten. Everyone thinks it's full of paintings and posh furniture. But the rooms Mrs T. made us wait in were all buckets and boxes of toilet rolls!

YOUR QUESTIONS ANSWERED

the Chancellor of the Exchequer, THE RT. HON. NIGEL LAWSON

Chancellor, how exactly does the Government's financial strategy work?

Well, putting it simply, imagine that there are two men, the first of whom has twelve apples. He decides to invest six in British Appletree, and of the seven that are remaining he donates three to the Conservative Party, which leaves him with five apples and a knighthood.

What about the second man?

Well, I'm glad you asked me that. Because he was too lazy to get himself some wealthy parents he only started with one apple, a bit of orange peel and three mouldy grapes. However, Sir First Man was kind enough to give him a job on his apple tree.

Hang on, Chancellor. How did Sir First Man . . .

– Lord First Man.

How did he get hold of the apple tree?

By working hard.

But doesn't the second man work hard?

Don't you want to ask about the Public Sector Borrowing Requirement?

No.

Well, it's quite simple: the Public Sector Borrowing Requirement . . .

Why are you spending so much on Defence?

Moving on now, the second man – remember him? – he's priced himself out of a job by making unrealistic demands on Lord First Man.

Such as?

Asking to be paid. But when Lord First Man makes him redundant he very generously gives him a Golden Delicious Handshake.

Eurgh. What use is that?

Well, if he invests it sensibly, he can get a jolly good return on it.

That reminds me. Why are interest rates so high?

Er . . . well of course . . . this is essential to keep down inflation, er . . . which, as we all know, was caused by the last Labour Government.

But if interest rates are high, people have to pay more for their mortgages, which pushes inflation up. Besides, you've been in power for nearly seven years now, and it's still going up.

Ha ha. Let's just stick to apples, shall we?

No. What happened to North Sea Oil?

Well, this had to go to fund Mr Second Man's dole apples. They don't grow on trees, you know.

But what causes all this unemployment?

Well, there are no easy answers . . .

Doesn't it all come back to high interest rates?

Shut up.

Where are those tax cuts you promised?

Next question.

Why did you just hit me?

Well, you see, hard times call for hard measures.

And finally, Chancellor . . .

Yes?

What is $(\sqrt{144} + 2^3) \div (4^2 - \sqrt{36})$*?*

Um . . . oooh . . . ah . . . well, the square root of 144 is 11. No it isn't. Crumbs . . . 2^3, that's 6 isn't it? Oh golly, where's my calculator? . . . equals 24 carry one, take away 3 from both sides . . . gosh, it's hot in here . . . minus 7 plus cos A minus the square of the hippopotamus . . . difficult to breathe, choke – gasp, 6 divided by Log 7. Oooer my head . . . what's happening? Aaaoorrggghhhh

CRITICS CHOICE

FILM WEST END

1) **'Ghostsbusters'**
Henrik Ibsen and Samantha Fox together at last in a box office smash.

2) **'The Bill Cotton Club'**
A tale of internecine strife among the upper echelons of the BBC.

3) **'Death Wish III'**
A documentary about British tourists in Spain.

4) **'Koyaanisqatsi'**
The wartime classic set in Morocco, starring Humphrey Bogart, Ingrid Bergman, Dooley Wilson and produced by the Guardian typesetters.

5) **'A Passage to Indiana Jones'**
Harrison Ford gets lost in the Malabar Caves and encounters the power-mad tyrant, David Lean.

THEATRE

1) **'No Sex Please We're Britons'** (Garrick)
A hilarious romp through the Roman Invasion by Howard Brenton.

2) **'Dozy Pulls It Off'**
Sir Geoffrey Howe succeeds in tying his shoelaces. Running time 3½ hours.

3) **'Two Into One'**
Norman Fowler's farcical suggestions to combat hospital overcrowding.

4) **'Whose Lesser God Is It, Anyway?'**
A moving drama concerning the cast's struggle against the cruel fact that Nature deprived them of the ability to act.

5) **'Joseph and the Amazing Technicolor Yawn'**
The Education Secretary has to be excused during a Cabinet meeting.

CABARET

1) **Tony Sound** (Mango Cabaret, Tues)
A healthy reaction against the traditional trappings of comedy – like dinner jackets, sexism and jokes. Don't miss his hilarious 'junkie flatmate' routine.

2) **The Embarrassment Brothers** (Upstairs at the Firetrap, Mon–Wed)
Sweeping away the old tenets of traditional joke-making and bullying the audience instead. Don't miss their hilarious 'flatmate on drugs' routine.

3) **Jenny Mennacrap** (The Bikeshed, Dalston, Mon, Wed, Thur)
A song, a smile, a joke about castration. If you don't laugh, you must be sexist.

4) **Johnny Rage** (Bungleurs, Battersea, Sat)
Angry poet. Angry because he can't fit all the words into the line. Don't miss his hilarious 'Ode to my Coked-up Flatmate'.

5) **Andy Righton** (Upstairs at the Royal Opera House, Covent Garden)
Your chance to see him live after his sell-out college tour; star of Channel 4's 'The Drain', BBC-2's 'Get With-It!' and now signed up with Goldcrest. Uncompromising jokes about his life on the dole. The second hour of the show consists of his now classic 'drugged-up flatmate' act.

6) **Barrie Bremner** (Blocked Lav at the Red Lion, Mon-Christmas)
Rising young impressionist with his take-offs of Tony Sound, the Embarrassment Brothers, Jenny Mennacrap, Johnny Rage, Andy Righton and Frank Spencer.

SINGLES

1) **Simon Le Bonbon: 'A View To A Diet'**
2) **Chas 'n' Dave: 'Dahn The Khazi'**
3) **The Smiths: 'Cheer Me Up, Someone'**
4) **Dire Straits: 'Hand Over Gold'**
5) **Frankie Goes to Hollywood: 'Two Chords'**
6) **Wham!: 'Wake Me Up Before The Record Stops'**
7) **Boy George and Culture Club: 'Do You Really Want To Listen To This?'**
8) **Marilyn: 'Ditto'**
9) **Prince: 'When Sparrows Fart'**
10) **Michael Jackson: 'Another Track From "Thriller"'**

TOP HOLE VIDEOS 237b Fulham Rd., SW10.

Come to THV where despite the changes in the law we can still supply you with the
STURDIEST FRANK, FOREIGN and ECCENTRIC!!!
~~STRONGEST~~ videos, strictly ~~EXPLICIT, EXOTIC~~ and KINKY!!!

Our videos guaranteed ~~UNCENSORED HARDCORE~~ ACTION!! No holds barred!
CREEPY, STARTLING AND RUNNING A SLIGHT TEMPERATURE!
Also many ~~HORROR~~ classics – ~~VIOLENT, GORY AND SICK! And we assure you~~

~~NO GOVERNMENT TAMPERING!!!~~

CURRENT STOCK

MARRIED LIFE
~~PORN~~
Telegraph
Give Us Our Daily ~~Sex~~
Pastry
Danish ~~Crumpet~~
Fanta
Last ~~Tango~~ in Paris
Voice Lee Marvin
Deep ~~Throat,~~ with ~~Linda Lovelace~~
The Story of Mother Theresa
~~Behind Convent Walls~~
Linguaphone
~~Private French Lessons~~
Waiting for the Right Girl
~~Rampant Homo Lovers~~

NOT QUITE NICES
~~VIDEO NASTIES~~
Drunken Dentist
~~Driller Killer~~
Wednesday the 4th
~~Friday the 13th~~
Misunderstood
The ~~Evil~~ Dead
Afternoon Vegetarians
~~Night~~ of the ~~Cannibals~~
Ant
Zombie ~~Flesh~~eaters
DP
S ~~S~~ Experimental Camp
Sussex Hedgeclipper Mishap
~~The Texas Chainsaw Massacre~~

If, like me, you want to be as dirty as you like but still look clean, try the new improved ZANU Party machine! It deals with smalls like Muzorewa and big stains on your sheet like UANC and Nkomo
HELLO Comrade Bob Here
Nearly 8 out of 10 voters said they preferred it. So I got rid of the other 2. ZANU – The ideal way to save power.
ZANU
HALF-COCK ECONOMY PROGRAMME!
HIGH SPEED CONDITIONING
ONE REVOLUTION – NO MORE NEEDED
THE MAKERS OF ZANU RECOMMEND
Purge
FOR A REALLY WHITE-WASH
ZANU THE APPLIANCE OF VIOLENCE
NOW! INSTANT CREDIBILITY. EASY TERMS OF OFFICE UP TO 1000 YEARS!

VOTE FOR
YOUR LABOUR CANDIDATE

~~REG FREESON~~ RED KEN

Dear Constituent

What Brent East deserves is a good left-wing MP with a solid record on all the main issues – unilateral disarmament, public ownership and anti-racism. But luckily we've managed to get rid of him so you've got me instead. Now, when I won the nomination for this seat, a lot of people accused me of duplicity, deviousness and self-interest. But these aren't the only qualities a good politician needs. He must also:

- Wear safari suits
- Be on TV a lot
- Visit Old People's flats.

A lot of the same people say I betrayed my colleagues on the GLC by voting for a legal rate. Well, to begin with I'm the Leader and in sensible politics everyone should do what the leader tells them to (see below). Secondly, in a democracy we must all uphold the rule of law. Otherwise they won't let you be an MP. And lastly, I was up against a Deputy who looked like stabbing me in the back and seizing the leadership for himself. And we can't have history repeating itself quite so soon, can we? Anyway, the quarrel's all patched up now and as for the GLC leadership – well mate, it's all yours.

Vote for me because I am confident I can win this constituency. It's progressive, it's multi-ethnic, and it's got a bloody huge Labour majority.

NEIL KINNOCK says

I think Red Ken is the best thing since sliced bread. He's thin, pasty, and lacking in substance. But above all, he knows which side he's buttered on. So I know Ken and I can work together in the Commons. He's dedicated, energetic, and has a terrific grasp of the chief political truth: people who hang around with Benn don't get jobs in the Cabinet.

And finally, I should like to refute any suggestion that Ken is some kind of "brown noser". He's just been sniffing around for a good seat.

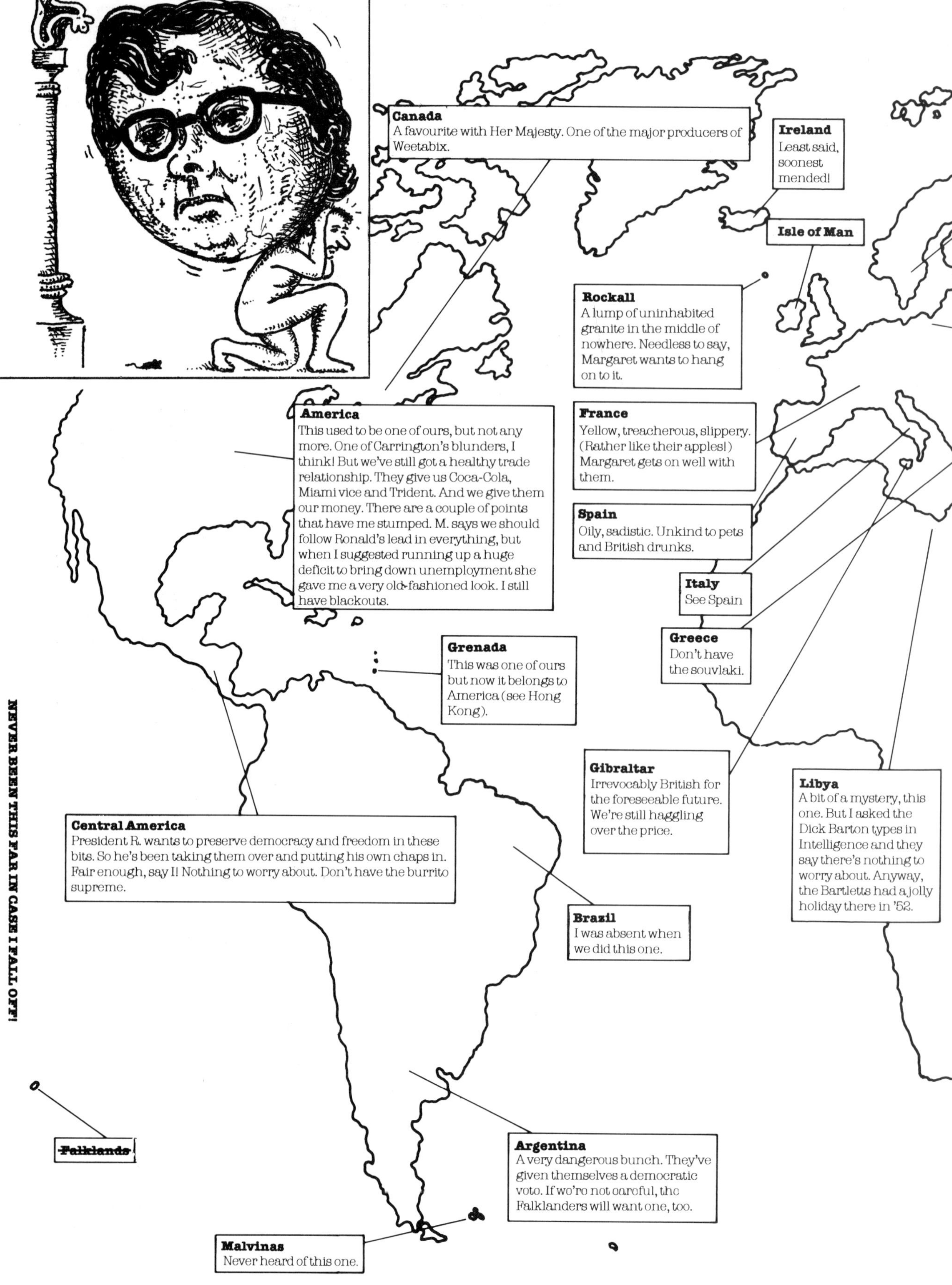
Canada
A favourite with Her Majesty. One of the major producers of Weetabix.
Ireland
Least said, soonest mended!
Isle of Man
Rockall
A lump of uninhabited granite in the middle of nowhere. Needless to say, Margaret wants to hang on to it.
America
This used to be one of ours, but not any more. One of Carrington's blunders, I think! But we've still got a healthy trade relationship. They give us Coca-Cola, Miami vice and Trident. And we give them our money. There are a couple of points that have me stumped. M. says we should follow Ronald's lead in everything, but when I suggested running up a huge deficit to bring down unemployment she gave me a very old-fashioned look. I still have blackouts.
France
Yellow, treacherous, slippery. (Rather like their apples!) Margaret gets on well with them.
Spain
Oily, sadistic. Unkind to pets and British drunks.
Italy
See Spain
Greece
Don't have the souvlaki.
Grenada
This was one of ours but now it belongs to America (see Hong Kong).
Gibraltar
Irrevocably British for the foreseeable future. We're still haggling over the price.
Libya
A bit of a mystery, this one. But I asked the Dick Barton types in Intelligence and they say there's nothing to worry about. Anyway, the Bartletts had a jolly holiday there in '52.
Central America
President R. wants to preserve democracy and freedom in these bits. So he's been taking them over and putting his own chaps in. Fair enough, say I! Nothing to worry about. Don't have the burrito supreme.
Brazil
I was absent when we did this one.
NEVER BEEN THIS FAR IN CASE I FALL OFF!
~~Falklands~~
Argentina
A very dangerous bunch. They've given themselves a democratic vote. If we're not careful, the Falklanders will want one, too.
Malvinas
Never heard of this one.

SIR GEOFFREY HOWE'S
Map of the World

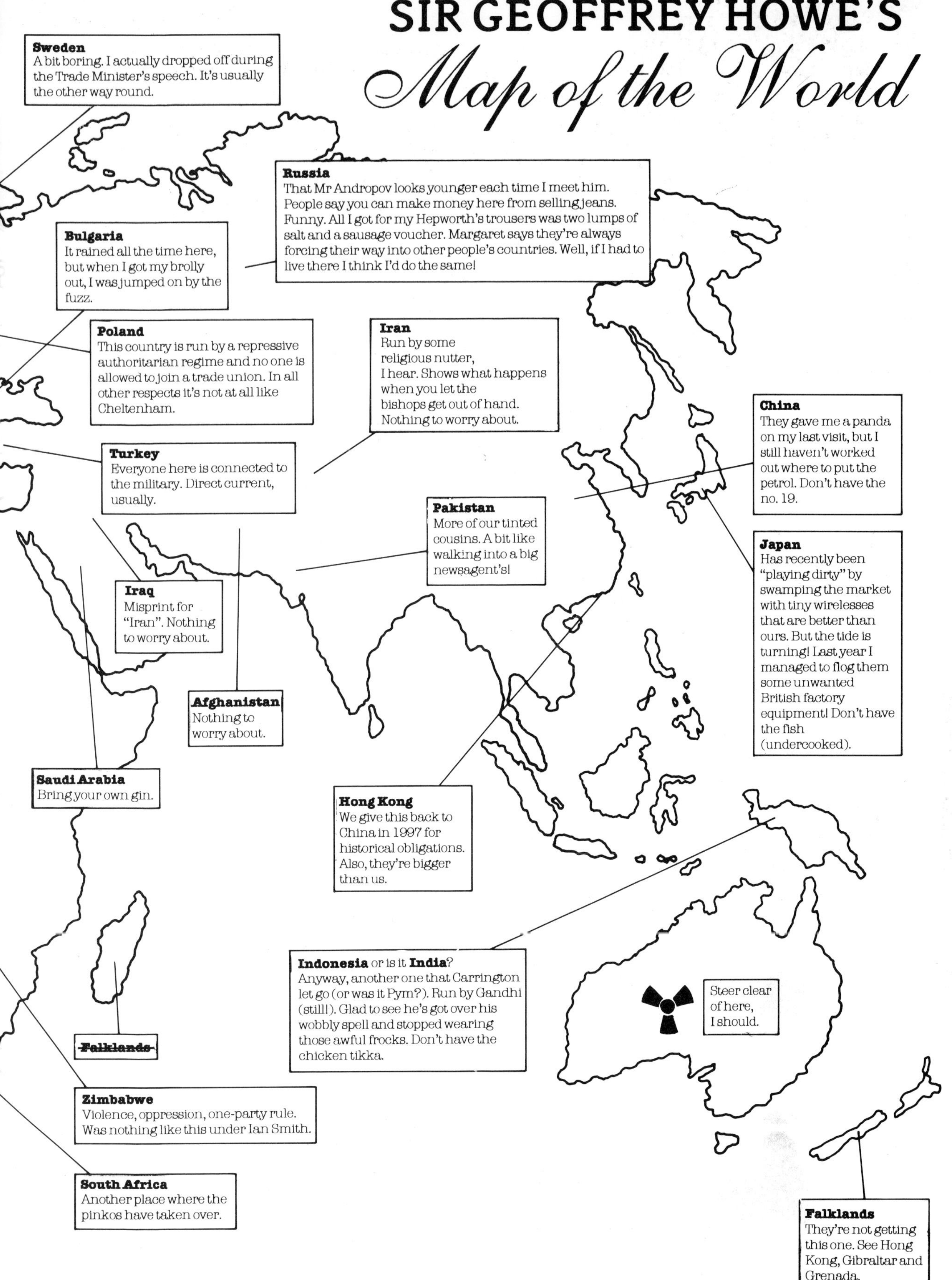

The National Theatre

was officially opened by the Queen on 25 October 1976, as soon as they had convinced her it was really finished.

It consists of three separate theatres: the **Olivier**, the **Lyttleton**, and the **Cottlesloe Bingo Centre**.

Apart from its main productions, the NT stages workshops (in which the actors weave baskets to raise money), regular platform performances from Sir Peter Hall threatening to resign, and readings by redundant staff of the bit in Sir Peter's Diaries where he votes Tory.

The National Theatre receives financial assistance from the Greater London Council and the Arts Council of Great Britain. One down, one to go.

The aims of the NT are to present classic, new, and neglected plays from the whole of world drama. Our next production is **Murder at the Vicarage** by Agatha Christie, a musical romp featuring Paul Shane (Ted Bovis of **Hi-De-Hi**) and with an all-singing, tap-dancing finale! Book now. Coach parties welcomed.

NT Patron:
Her Majesty The Queen

KING LEAR

a new adaptation enforced by the Government cuts.

This production was made possible by The Blue Peter Appeal, 1985. Thanks for the ringpulls, everyone!

Lear, King of Britain	**Sir Peter Hall**
King of France	**Sir Peter Hall**
Duke of Burgundy	**Sir Peter Hall (if I can get changed in time)**
Duke of Albany	**Someone from the audience**
Earl of Kent	**His Friend**
Earl of Gloucester	**Someone else from the audience**
Edgar, son to Gloucester	**Oh dear, we've run out of Audience**
Edmund, Bastard son to Gloucester	**Lord Gowrie**
Curan, a Courtier	**Archie Andrews**
Oswald, Steward to Goneril	**An Action Man on the end of a pole**
Old Man	**Sir Peter Hall in a "Mr T" mask**
Fool	**Sir Peter Hall with his back to the audience**
Goneril Regan Cordelia	**The Ice Cream Lady**

Other parts played by members of the **7th Lambeth Cub Scouts**

Director	**Me again**
Set designed and built by	**Class 2b, St Bride's Infant School**
Costumes	**The Blind Shop**
Lighting	**Hole in the Roof**
Music	**Radio 3 up loud**

Production credits
Wardrobe care by Rent-a-skip. Begging bowl by Heal's. Armour by Hamleys Catering by the Salvation Army

There will be one interval. Latecomers will not be re-admitted unless they buy an ice cream.

1

2

3

Sir Peter Hall (Director, Lear, France, Burgundy, Old Man, Fool) Sir Peter has had many brilliant productions during his directorship of the NT including: *The Ring* (Bayreuth), *A Midsummer-Night's Dream* (Glyndebourne), *The Marriage of Figaro* (Glyndebourne), but nevertheless has managed to squeeze in the odd job for the National. TV appearance: Fat, bearded, huge bags under the eyes.

Lord Gowrie (Bastard)
Grey Gowrie has been Mrs Thatcher's Minister of Arts since 1983, but despite this has a keen interest in culture. As a discriminating aesthete he will only wipe his bottom on the works of Gerard Manley Hopkins. Many collections of poetry published including: *The Loom of Life* (Gowrie Press), *Laughter and Tears* (Gowrie Publications), *Joy and Heartache* (Gowrie & Gowrie), *Some More of Me Poetry!* (Gowrie House), *Report on Overmanning at the National Theatre* (HMSO).

Someone From The Audience (Albany)
Many West End appearances include: *Man in Front of You Who Keeps Moving His Head* (Haymarket), *Chap in Seat T17 with an Irritating Cough* (Aldwych), *Person Eating an Everlasting Supply of Individually Wrapped Nuttall's Mintoes* (Coliseum), *Latecomer with a Squeaky Leather Coat and Two Big Plastic Bags* (Royal Exchange, Manchester), *Idiot Who Laughs Very Loudly in the Wrong Places During Something by Strindberg* (Nottingham Playhouse), *The Cretin with the Digital Watch That Beeps Every Half Hour* (Royal Festival Hall). Someone from the Audience appears by courtesy of His Friend who climbed in through the lavatory window and pushed open the Exit Bar.

1 Lord Gowrie in rehearsal
2 Action Man
3 Someone From The Audience

During the interval, why not try a **Losely Park Ice Cream?** We have a wide selection of *outré* flavours such as Minnesota Fudge Sorbet, Kiwi Fruit Ripple, Crystallised Guava, Camomile Butter, Banana and Salmon, Bread Fruit and Stem Ginger, Orchid Pollen and Ginseng.

Bookshop

The National Theatre bookshop carries a comprehensive stock of definitive theatrical texts, i.e. Peter Hall's Diaries (authenticated by Hugh Trevor-Roper).

Also available are posters, postcards, teeshirts, badges, stickers, "Kiss-me-quick" Hats, Snoopy Mugs, plastic policemen's helmets, Big Ben keyrings, Garfield tea-towels, Peter Hall pyjama cases.

National Theatre, South Bank, London SE1 9PX

Telephone:
01-928-2252 to be told that all the tickets have been bought up by agents to be sold to gullible Americans.

Please leave your coats in the free cloakroom in the entrance foyer under the sign "Bring and Buy".

The NT's underground car park is the bit without the carpet.

Two of the costume designs for this production

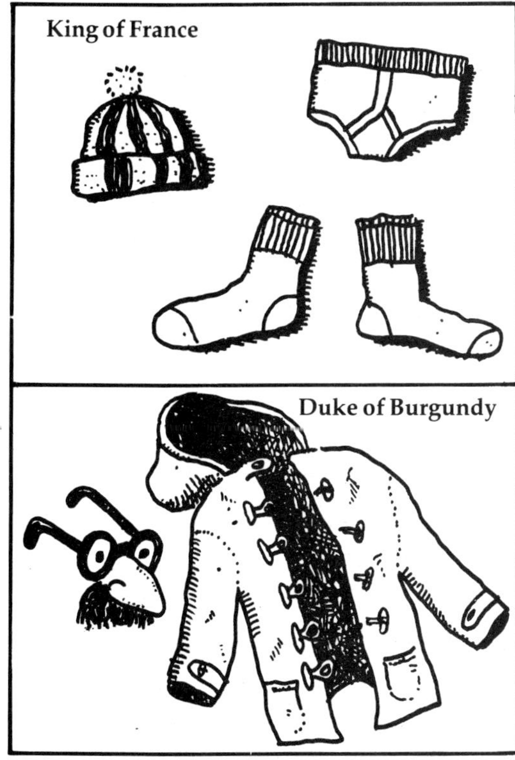

A copy of this poster is available in the foyer. Price £5.75

Daily Mail COMMENT

Britain on the Road to Recovery

YES, it's official – Doctor Thatcher has pulled us through. The CBI says output, orders and exports are up, up, up.

In Cowley, they're building Maestros as quickly as people are buying them. And after lunch, even quicker!

Sales of foreign cars are falling too. A man in Stevenage has refused to buy a Toyota. Good for you, chum! While in Germany somebody's bought that food-mixer we sent.

The rosy dawn of recovery also shines on South Wales where they've even started *opening* steel works. What splendid job-centres they make too!

Yes, everything is up, up, up. The CBI is touching figures UP. The corners of Maggie's mouth are UP. The odds on me getting a peerage are UP.

So, there you have it. Britain is on the Road to Recovery. Maggie, you're the tops!

Dodd's on favourite

ON his 55th birthday surely Mr Ken Dodd merits some recognition. Why, even Mrs Thatcher rates him as her favourite laughter-maker.

And who better to judge than this remarkable lady, who has fought and won wars in the South Atlantic, the Coal Fields and the EEC.

No accolade is too great for a man who has so selflessly served his leader. (See what I'm getting at? – Sir D.E.)

Arise, Lord Ken of Knotty Ash.

The Red Sky Pilots Who Hi-jack The Faith

SMASH THESE BRAZEN IDLES!

by JOHN SELWYN GUMMER MP

RIGHT! RIGHT! Stop what you're doing and read this article!

I expect like me you're jolly well browned off with all these bishops who mix religion and politics. It reminds me of when the Prime Minister started her term of office by quoting St Francis of Assisi: "Where there is discord may we bring harmony. Where there is strife may we bring tranquillity. Where there is high unemployment may we bring a mobile exhibition about starting your own computer business."

All right! I know I am a member of Synod. But it's not because I'm a politician. It's because I swotted blinking hard at school and came third in Div.

Where was I? Oh yes – Bishops! In particular the Bishop of blooming Durham! Why doesn't he start behaving like a proper bishop – umpiring the village cricket, driving a Morris Minor and doing the magic show for the Christmas party?

Claptrap

I'm a reasonable man. You have to be when you've been Chairman of the Cambridge University Conservative Union. And I was Secretary of the Christian Union (or "God Squad" as we used to call it! We don't mind a joke! And neither does God). And I played "Policeman 4" in Selwyn College's production of "The Pirates of Penzance".

Anyway. To return to Durham Dave. Oh – and Treasurer of the Ballroom Dancing Society. Where in the Bible does it say you have to be nice to people? And don't say "The Good Samaritan" because I did that one for my fifth form project! Put *that* in your censer and swing it bishop!

You see, no-one would have remembered the Good Samaritan if he hadn't had *money*. Money which he gave to a poor person...no, wait. He didn't give it to a poor person. He took the poor person to an inn and told the landlord to put everything on the slate. Oooh, cripes, that's borrowing, isn't it? No, well, probably what happened was that the poor person had comprehensive medical insurance at very reasonable rates, I should think.*

Success

Oh well, never mind about the Good Samaritan.

What about the pensioner that Our Saviour told to pick up his bed and walk? Not an NHS doctor in sight. And even on the Cross Our Lord was preaching the virtues of self-reliance and initiative. Three days later he was off his backside and out looking for work!

And now after a mere two thousand years he's worked his way to the head of an international business with branches in every major city. So the Lord has a very real message for us: "These are my policies, and to hell with the Opposition." Ha!

*I know this because I did Business Studies at S-level. Also I've got French A-level which is blinking hard. And eleven O-levels, which Mother said at the time was quite unusual. *And* one of them was Greek, for which I had to have an extra period in the lunch hour.

John Selwyn Gummer is something in the Conservative Party and a freelance prat.

TODAY'S POEMS Selected by Kingsley Amis

My first choice is a recently discovered fragment of Chaucer describing a health minister's intention to bring the NHS kicking and screaming into the 14th century.

The Mynysteres Tale

Ther was a Clark, hight Kennethe of Westmynyster,
Who had a plan, that others thoghte right synyster;
To give thos patients from the Naciounall Healthe
Goode privy treatment – though with publicke wealthe.
The reason was, yoonge master Kennethe seyde,
Swich privy wings oft hadde an extra bedde;
Hir quaakes and operaciouns cost less plate
Than those engendered by the Welfar Staat.
But those that herde this pondered ashen-lypped,
And asked if Kennethe hadde y-byscuitte slypped.
For had nat many a Haarlie-Strete addresse
Grown riche by spongynge off the NHS?
And had nat quaakes and surgeonnes filled hir purse
While publicke money paid to train the nurse?
In soothe, we'll trust what master Kennethe preaches
When patients suck the bloode from the leeches.

Kingsley Amis was one of Britain's best loved poem-choosers until the Daily Mirror worked out that anyone could do it for a tenth of the price. Funnily enough, Amis used to be a writer himself and indeed once wrote a novel! Though some more sceptical critics suggest that this was a piece of juvenilia from his more brilliant son, Martin. Having commenced his career as a left-wing firebrand Kingsley moved ever further to the right until by the time of his demise he was working for Robert Maxwell.

And now two pieces by Margaret Savage Thatcher, one of the new generation of "ranting" poets. The first conveys her anger at her critics or "cuckoos". As she said at one of her readings: "Mr. Speaker, I suppose we should always expect to hear cuckoos at this time of year." Unfortunately it was November.

Lhude Sing Cuccu! (or Gummer is Icumen In)

Hail to thee, blithe Spirit!
As Keats said in his ode,
When welcoming the cuckoo
That in his garden crowed.
The cuckoos I've been hearing
Are terribly confused,
But don't they like this weather?
As Coleridge once mused.
My critics in the Commons
Turn logic on its head,
So, cuckoo, shall I call them?
As Robert Browning said.
They get their facts all muddled,
Which really makes me cross;
It's worse than being lumbered
With Kipling's albatross:
That's why I call out "cuckoo!"
When people get things wrong,
And I hail them, like Byron,
Or was it Patience Strong?

But anger is only one arrow in Thatcher's quiver. She also has a very well developed sense of pride. Here is her "Paean to Me" written on her 10th year as Tory leader.

Paean to Me

Ten years as leader! Two elections won!
Four million jobs, and more pounds sterling lost!
There's even days when Denis says "Well done!"
And then I see he's got his fingers crossed.
Thank goodness other people were inept:
Hats off to Michael Foot, that trembling voice
Made Tory politicians look adept,
And God bless Galtieri – Yes, "Rejoice!"
Thanks go to Ronnie, Nancy's lesser-half,
For making me look socially aware;
Thanks, Neil, I loved that seaside photograph,
And, Davids both, you've stumbled here and there.
In fact, praise be to famous men who trip,
Do grant me ten more years of leadership.

The job of the Poet Laureate is to cheer up the people on occasions of national importance. Here is Ted Hughes' offering on the 40th anniversary of V.E. Day.

V.E. Day

The black outs came down today
London's putrid entrails
Spilled on pavements,
Lit, like afterbirth, by unaccustomed light.
Guts, puke, sweat, Vera Lynn.

It was a day of joyfulness,
But
The chasm of loneliness rang,
As death's rattle
Echoed around its chambers.
Blood, filth, venom, Larry the Lamb.

Relief was everywhere.
Relief the war was over.
Relief a lover's returned.
However, relief's not everything.
Ruins, bile, scar, V. E. Day.

WORLDWIDE INTERACTIVE NUCLEAR DISARMAMENT

Welcome to a new concept in international statesmanship.

Are you ever frustrated at the way ordinary people like you have no say in important decisions that affect the world's future, like disarmament, food distribution and the axeing of *Dr Who*? Are you ever angry when you are deliberately excluded from all those talks going on in Geneva? Yes? Well, now you can change all that. We at Interactive Superpower Publications offer you the chance to discover what it's like to lead, yes, lead a world superpower, be it Russia, America or BBC1. You can be the first kid on your bloc to take the step-by-step decisions in the complex process of Arms Reduction. Worldwide Interactive Nuclear Disarmament starts here!

Choose whether you wish to be President Reagan, Premier Gorbachev or Michael Grade.

President Reagan
Go to A

Premier Gorbachev
Go to Я

Michael Grade
Go to Page 625

A

How the West Pulled a Fast One

You awake with a start. You are Ronald Reagan. (Unless you are Nancy Reagan, in which case you awake with a jerk.) No, you are Ronald Reagan. Remember your Self Awareness Classes. You know, when you had to sit staring at the name on your AmEx card for five weeks.

You have three things of which you are most proud: your wife (Nancy, remember?), your children, and your own hair. Shame the colour belongs to someone else. Oh yes, and you are president of the most powerful nation on earth. Try to remember that bit. It means you have to stop watching those Audie Murphy videos now and then.

Today is a big day. It is a day of decision. You are going to decide whether to shave, go back to sleep or declare war on Russia.

Shave
Go to C

Sleep
Go to B

Declare War on Russia
Go to L

Я

Tsar Wars

You awake with a start. You are Mikhail Sergeyevich Gorbachev. You are young, dynamic and go-ahead. 'Oooor,' you exclaim in your bright, youthful manner. 'Fetch me my cardigan and slippers.'

You notice the insistent humming of your solid-state teasmade as she pushes a glass of hot water under your nose and goes off to scrub the potatoes.

'Where's the tea bag?' you enquire turning to your lovely young wife Raisa, who is seductively waxing her upper lip.

'She's gone to scrub the potatoes,' comes the groovy reply.

'Very funny. But,. Raisa, I thought tea bag production was on target this year.'

'It is, but we used them both yesterday,' answers your gamine bedmate.

Struggling up the steep gradient away from her side of the mattress, you make a mental note to stamp out corruption in the Tea Bag Collectives of Tomsk. You brace yourself and tiptoe across the bedroom's deep-pile marble floor, while your swish, Italian-style dentures rattle trendily in their sockets.

'Now, where's my Lada-tronic Peopleshave Razor, my slinky little sable?'

'Ogh sorry, Mikky, I've just broken February's blade on my legs.'

You are angry. Do you storm off to the breakfast room for a bowl of wheat? Or do you go for a relaxing stroll into Finland with half a million close friends?

Breakfast
Go to Б

Finland
Go to Л

Б

The V. I. Lenin Hall of Breakfast is just down the corridor, a brief troika ride away. What will breakfast be today? Cabbage? A mixed grill of bacon, eggs, tomato and sausage? Devilled kidneys and kedgeree? Flapjacks and maple syrup? Your mouth waters as you open the salver. It's cabbage.

'Ho hum,' you sigh. 'Victory to the People.'

At that moment, Raisa bustles through on her way out, looking the picture of elegance in her mink donkey-jacket and her white leather hobnails.

'Can I have the car today, Mikky?' she booms.

'Oh, sorry, I promised to lend it to Lithuania.' You open the paper. 'Nothing but lies in Pravda *these days.'*

An impish dimple appears on your wife's cheek. 'Then perhaps, Mikhail, you should stop writing them. Tyoodle pyip! I'm off to work.'

You laugh ironically. 'Don't fall into the smelter, my Archangelsk.'

With a 'Mush!' and a yapping of huskies she is away.

Your turn now. What's your plan for today? Work or recreation?

Work	**Recreation**
Go to Ц	Go to Г

B

'Zzzzzzzzzzzzzzzzzzzzzzzzzz zzzzzzzzzzzzzzzzzzzzzzzzzz zzzzzzzzzzzzzzzzz Not now, Nancy. I'm writing a speech. Zzzzzzzzzzzzzzzzzzz zzzzzzzzzzzzzzzzzzzzzzzzzzz zzzzzzzzzzzzzzzzzzzzzzzzzzz zzzzzzzzmmzmmmmzmmm mmmmmmmzzzz mmmmmm bbbbbssssbbbbssssbbb sssss sssssssyyyy¾vvvvvvmmmvv ccc%%½%%-½i%Aaamn aaaaaamamammmannnnnn ????ZZddddiuuuuGeorge, for God's sake, fix the auto-prompt zzzzzzzzzzzzzzzzzzz zzzzzzzzz Thanks zzzzzzzzz zzzzzzzzzzzzzzzzzzzzzzzzzz zzzzDown, Trigger!zzzz.'

You wake up. If you are in bed, go to C

If you are in your office, go to F

C

You get up. Now for the big one. Can you find the bathroom by yourself? It's a cinch! You take a leak and set about those whiskers with the electric razor.

'Hey, Ronnie,' comes your wife's mellifluous squawk. 'What are you doing with the coffee-grinder?'

Suddenly you are in the kitchen.

'I thought it was a closer shave than usual,' you say.

Nancy passes you a box of Scotties. 'Sit down,' she says, 'You look like an Agent Orange victim.'

As you both laugh and you dab your shredded jowl, you admire your wife's dexterity in painting her toenails, doing her aerobics and eating a Lo-fat yoghurt simultaneously.

'Say, Nancy, I love your new face-lift!'

'Ron-nee! I'm bending over!'

'Uh-huh.' Suki, your Vietnamese boatperson pours you a mug of coffee. You take a sip. 'Nancy, I've just remembered where I took that leak.'

Your wife gives you a long look from between her knees. 'I think it's time you had a holiday.'

'Yeah, we haven't had a holiday since I-don't-know-when.'

'Tuesday,' ripostes Nancy, clenching her instep firmly between her teeth. 'Let's get out to the ranch as soon as we can.'

'But, honey. This afternoon is my day at the office. What shall I do?'

What indeed, Ron? The ranch or the office? Holiday or work? These decisions are made every day by the most powerful man on earth.

Holiday	**Work**
Go to D	Go to F

D

Yes! You are on holiday! And speeding along in the limo towards your Santa Monica ranch, you catch a glimpse of the verdant countryside through the chink in the FBI men. Your heart beats a little faster as their walkie-talkies interfere with your pacemaker. You muse on the greatness of the United States of Am-Am-Am-Amnesia. Land of the Strong – if you're on Medicare. Home of the Brave – so long as he stays on his reservation. You step out for a second to stretch your legs and – whooaaaaaaaaah! The car screeches to a halt half a mile up the road and reverses to meet you. Your whole life begins to flash past your eyes before the husky ex-astronauts pick you up.

'Not so fast, boys,' you protest. 'I'm only up to 1952: *Squadron of Valor* – one of my best!'

Eventually the car crosses the small creek marking the entrance to your ranch. The bridge groans under the weight of the motorcade, constructed as it is from a cantilevered arrangement of ex-Welfare Claimants. 'Let the State be a burden on them for a change,' you quip, looking round to see if any reporters have taken this down.

As soon as you get in, you open the icebox for a cold beer, only to find it filled with gifts from your last trip to South Korea – twelve photogenic children.

Three days later Nancy arrives, slightly breathless, takes off her training shoes and flops down into a Nautilus machine.

'I'm glad you're here, Nancy,' you say. 'It's time to go.'

'But, Ron-nee,' she sweetly whines, 'You said you wanted some quiet music. So I've got Frank Sinatra and Nelson Riddle to play some of their hits on the other side of the lake.'

What should you do? Listen to Frank and the boys? Go back to the office? Or watch old Audie Murphy videos on TV?

Office	**TV**	**Sinatra**
Go to F	Go to E	Go to K

Г

You have chosen a day of fun: a visit to the Nikita Khrushchev State Psychiatric Hospital. You are met on arrival by Dr I. N. Lunebin, Chief Clinician, Professor of Psychiatry and Colonel in the KGB.

'Welcome, Comrade Chairman,' he says, compassionately removing his knuckle-dusters to shake hands with you. 'We have some fascinating cases to show you today. Come in to the J. V. Stalin High Security Ward for the Socially Maladjusted.'

You pass through the Occupational Therapy Unit, where rehabilitated patients are shovelling salt in readiness for the part they'll play in the community outside.

'Here we are,' smiles the doctor. 'Look at this poor soul. He has terrible difficulty sleeping.'

'How come?'

'We keep waking him up. And Ivan over here, he thinks the KGB keep following him around.'

'And they don't, of course.'

'No. Not now we've got him where we can see him.'

You both chuckle compassionately. There is a crackle of static and a grateful scream as revolutionary strides are made in Electro-Convulsive Therapy. Dr Lunebin explains: 'We simply pass a current through the patient's disturbed brain.'

'Oh,' you ponder, 'but what's it doing down there?'

'All power to the Gulags!' he quips.

'I see, but these people aren't mad. They're just dissidents.'

The good doctor's eyes light up. 'Aha! But everyone knows dissidents end up in here. Therefore, if you become a dissident, you must be mad.'

Suddenly all becomes clear. You congratulate Lunebin on his wonderful healing work and ask him if there's any way you can help.

'Since you come to mention it,' he says. 'There's the small matter of the electricity bill.'

You make an excuse and go to Ц.

E

Ooops! The remote control on your TV coincidentally has the same frequency as the signal which activates the entire nuclear arsenal of the United States of America.

Go to L

Ц

You arrive at the Politburo staggering and out of breath. You always do this as a demonstration of fraternity with your colleagues. There they are round the Laika the Dog Memorial Oak Slab, seated stiffly to attention in their solid walnut chairs. Perhaps Comrade General Geriatrikev is a little too *stiff. But no matter. Comrade Gromyko – never far from every Soviet Premier's elbow just in case their knees give way – is the first to speak.*

'Well Comrade, what is your first Five Year Plan?'

'Lasting longer than five years,' you think to yourself as you trot out a load of platitudes about stamping out alcoholism to counter the alarming fall in vodka production. 'And then, Gromyko, I want you to crack down on corruption.'

'Da, da,' *says the unbuyable Grandfather of the Revolution. 'But it'll cost you.'*

Just then the door rumbles open and one of the young acolytes of the Foreign Secretariat breezes in in his Lada-matic bath chair.

'Yes?'

'The Great Enemy of the People's Struggle has proposed a major arms reduction,' chirps the wizened youth. A deathly silence falls across the table, as indeed does Comrade Geriatrikev.

'Very well,' you intone with all the dignity of your office. 'Send him a full and considered reply. You'll find a pile of rejection slips in the basement.'

'Nyet, nyet,' *interjects Gromyko, the steadfast Brother-in-Law of the Workers' Liberation, 'I have a better idea. Why not call the Tsarist Film star's bluff and agree to meet him at the U.N. He'll have to refuse and we'll appear to be the peacemakers.'*

So what's it to be? Do you reject Reagan's offer? Or do you take up the suggestion of the First Step-Cousin Twice Removed of the Victory of the Proletariat?

Reject offer
Go to ю

Meet at U.N.
Go to Ж

F

It's 2pm. You are in your office, ready for the full day's work ahead. You had no trouble finding your way to the Oval Room because it's the one without the corners. But your first task is to read a few letters. Well done! Today you have reached the letter 'D'. The door opens and in walks a worried Defense Secretary Caspar Weinberger. 'Hullo George,' you greet him. 'What's eating you?'

He explains that Congress has once again rejected your plans to destroy the credibility of the Nicaraguan government and sign them up for a TV mini-series.

'Aw, spit. How long before we can get rid of these damn communists?' you ask.

'Well, Mr President. Our boys in Managua are doing their–'

'No, Ed, you meathead,' you intervene. 'I meant Congress.'

At that moment, in bursts George Bush, or is it Schultz? You can never remember.

'Hi Donald,' you say.

'Mr President,' he gasps, 'the Soviets have proposed a major arms reduction.'

'Well that's just swell,' you say, cocking your head jauntily.

'No it isn't,' replies George. Or is it Ed? 'They want us to do it as well.'

An inarticulate whimper escapes from the back of your throat. You have a sudden flashback of the day Mom had your puppy put down for committing miscegenation.

'And what's worse,' continues the guy you're talking to, 'Gorbachev's proposed you meet him at the U.N. in six weeks' time.'

'What do I do, guys? What do I do?'

The two aides fix you with a stare. 'No, Mr President. *You* have to decide.'

Do you reject Gorbachev's offers? Or do you make full use of the six weeks to find out where the U.N. is?

Reject offer
Go to G

Meet at U.N.
Go to H

Ю

Using the newly installed Hotline, you reject the American offer to impromptu applause, cheers and military parades from your colleagues. Nevertheless, you realize that America has raced ahead of you in weapons research riding on the backs of its manacled slave classes and you consider the fact that Russia's entire defence system depends on a Pacman machine smuggled out of a Herne Bay amusement arcade.

'We must press on with negotiations,' you announce.

There is a disgruntled wheezing from the 24 generals around the table, led by Comrade General Chestikov. You pick up the bakelite Lada-com receiver of the Superpower Hotline and put a transfer-charge call through to Washington. The Politburo passes a motion commending your thrift.

Acutely aware of the fourteen and a half pairs of ears hanging onto your every word, you make your offer to the Icon of Ruling Class Oppression: 'Halt your research into Star Wars,' you say, 'and we'll let you win on the Asymmetrical Bars next Olympics.'

You hear a hand being placed over the mouthpiece 10,000 miles away, a muffled voice saying, 'What are Asymmetrical Bars?', confused hubbub, and finally the voice of the pampered warlord saying, 'We agree.' Comrade General Chestikov has a seizure. 'But only if you remove your medium-range missiles from west of the Urals.'

A typical bourgeois trick.

Bearing in mind that you have 1,671 warheads concealed in a diplomatic bag in Highgate, London, do you accept, or do you refuse?

Accept **Refuse**
Go to Й Go to Λ

I

You accept Gorbachev's offer, and pull Cruise out of Europe. While you are at it, you halt Star Wars research, disarm MX, withdraw your troops from Central America, the Mediterranean and even the USA. You renounce the faith and establish a state-run economy based on mutual need and the ability to pay.

Go to Я

З

You accept Reagan's proposal and remove all medium-range weapons west of the Urals. For good measure you also deactivate all medium-range missiles east of the Urals. The long-range ones, too. You pull out your forces from Afghanistan, Poland, East Germany, and even the U.S.S.R. You invent a safe method of leaving this planet altogether, but not before you are converted to Christian capitalism.

Go to A

J

You reject Gorbachev's proposal, yet you are still aware of the increasing urgency of detente and further negotiation. You lean back pensively in your Presidential Leather Bathchair. You say: 'Aw fuck it, I'm 73. Let's get it over with,' and press a button marked 'GO FOR IT'.

Go to L

K

Bad luck! It turns out Frankie and the Boys are in fact a crack Iranian suicide squad with a long-range rocket launcher concealed in the brass section.

You are assassinated. You are now dead.

Go to F

Λ

You refuse Reagan's offer. The next day, a valve blows in Russia's Lada-pute Defence Computer.

Go to Л

Н

'So this is Denver,' you say to yourself as you stand in the lobby of the U.N. Building. Nancy is at your side, cuddling two black toddlers. The doors open and you cast an approving eye over the broad shoulders and firm jaw of the Soviet premier. But why is he wearing a skirt?

'Have you met my wife, Raisa?' asks a stocky Ernest Borgnine lookalike who then hugs you warmly and crushes your portable autoprompt. Without any hesitation he pinpoints the gaps in your briefing and asks you how you are.

You glance at the miniature screen which is now displaying last season's baseball scores, and are forced to resort to one of your best ad libs. 'Aw gee...I guess...um...well.'

As Nancy and the guy in the skirt go off on women's business, you chew the fat with the Evil Emperor. 'Mr Reagan, I come here in the hope that together we may heal the scars.'

'Aw, forget it, Darth. It was just a little accident with a coffee grinder.'

At last you fix your autoprompt and the serious negotiating begins.

Ж

You arrive at the U.N. building, New York, after a taxi-ride which costs you the Gross National Product of the Ukraine. 'Have a nice day,' groans the toiling slave of Western Monopoly Capitalism. You reach the main entrance and hold the double doors open for your luscious wife and her trolley-load of video machines, perfumes and Johnny Cash records. The Great Enemy of the People is there to greet you in person.

'How are you, Mr President?' you say, tempering your revolutionary zeal.

'Aw gee...I guess...um...well,' comes the statesman-like reply as he feverishly twiddles with his portable autoprompt.

'That must be your First Lady,' you remark as Nancy whisks your wife off for a Perrier jacuzzi.

'No,' he answers, 'that's Nancy. You're thinking of Jane Wyman.'

Then at last the serious negotiation begins.

'Before we do anything we must determine how many missiles each side has got.'

'Agreed. How many have you got?'

'Two.'

'Two?'

'That's right.'

'Then how come our satellite photographs show 6,794?'

'Er...dust on the lens.'

'I see.'

'How many have you got?'

'...One.'

'Are you sure?'

'Yes.'

'But our surveillance equipment detected 9,000.'

'They must have counted the same one 9,000 times.'

'Oh.'

'Still, perhaps you'd like to try some of this. We call it coffee.'

'We do have *coffee in the Soviet Union, you know. There's a very fine bush in the Leningrad Botanical Gardens.'*

'Sure. How many sugars?'

'6,794 – er – two.'

After 25 minutes of gruelling dialogue you reach an agreement.

Is it an agreement substantially to reduce your nuclear arsenal? Or do you agree to go on holiday and meet again in six months?

Reduce Go to I

Meet Again Go to D

After 25 minutes of invigorating dialectic you reach an agreement.

Is it an agreement substantially to reduce your nuclear arsenal? Or do you agree to take a relaxing break and meet again in six months?

Reduce Go to 3

Meet Again Go to Г

G

You have rejected the Russian offer.

But you realize that such a rejection could be harmful to America's peacemaking image, through your sound grasp of public opinion and because George, Caspar and Ed keep telling you so. Consequently you come up with a brilliant idea of your own (well, George's actually): make them an offer they have to refuse.

You again pick up the newly installed International Hotline, fired with enthusiasm, and have a long and fruitful discussion with Claudia Cardinale.

After a cold bath, you call the Kremlin. 'Remove your medium-range missiles from west of the Urals,' you tell them, shooting straight from the hip replacement, 'or we'll cancel Prince's tour of Russia.'

There is a stunned silence. Then the godless tyrant's voice is heard: 'We agree.' Your pacemaker skips a bleep. 'On condition that you withdraw Cruise from Europe.'

Commie plays dirty again.

Bearing in mind that Belgium's new Coke-bottling plant is in fact a Pershing Missile silo: do you accept, or do you refuse?

Accept Go to I

Refuse Go to J

Й

You wake up with a jolt. Dr I. N. Lunebin of the Nikita Khrushchev State Psychiatric Hospital has just passed a compassionate 2,000 volts through your lower brain.

'This is our star patient,' he explains to the new Soviet Premier, Comrade Gromyko. 'He was caught sealing an agreement with a leading member of the CIA.'

'Who was that?' inquires Gromyko's svelte new wife, Raisa.

'President Reagan.' Dr Lunebin leers in sympathy at you through his pebble glasses. 'Raise the voltage, Tanya.'

GAME OVER.
YOU LOSE.

L Л

WAR! This is what you've been working so hard for all these years.

All 10,000 Russian ICBMs are launched. A major triumph for Soviet technology: 943 work!

America launches hers. She keeps her promise to consult the British Government and posts them a letter.

The destruction of Britain's cities is so complete that the Environment Secretary promises each one a new Sports Centre. While in Downing Street's private shelter, the whole Cabinet is killed in the fight to hold the door open for Margaret Thatcher.

The Cruise missiles launched from RAF Greenham Common land on the HQ of Ratepayers Against the Greenham Encampments.

Another bomb lands in Australia – 5,000 British troops are moved in to test the effects.

90 per cent of Americans refuse to accept their death until it is confirmed by Barbara Walters on TV.

Only the people of Switzerland are saved by their prudent shelter-building programme, while millions in other countries commit suicide rather than face a world run by the Swiss.

The destruction is complete.

Arms Talks continue.

GAME OVER.
YOU LOSE.

Go to meet your maker

WORLDWIDE **I**NTERACTIVE **N**UCLEAR **D**ISARMAMENT

People who have no experience of world politics may find the preceding exchanges difficult to follow. To help you, here is the guide produced for Ronald Reagan.

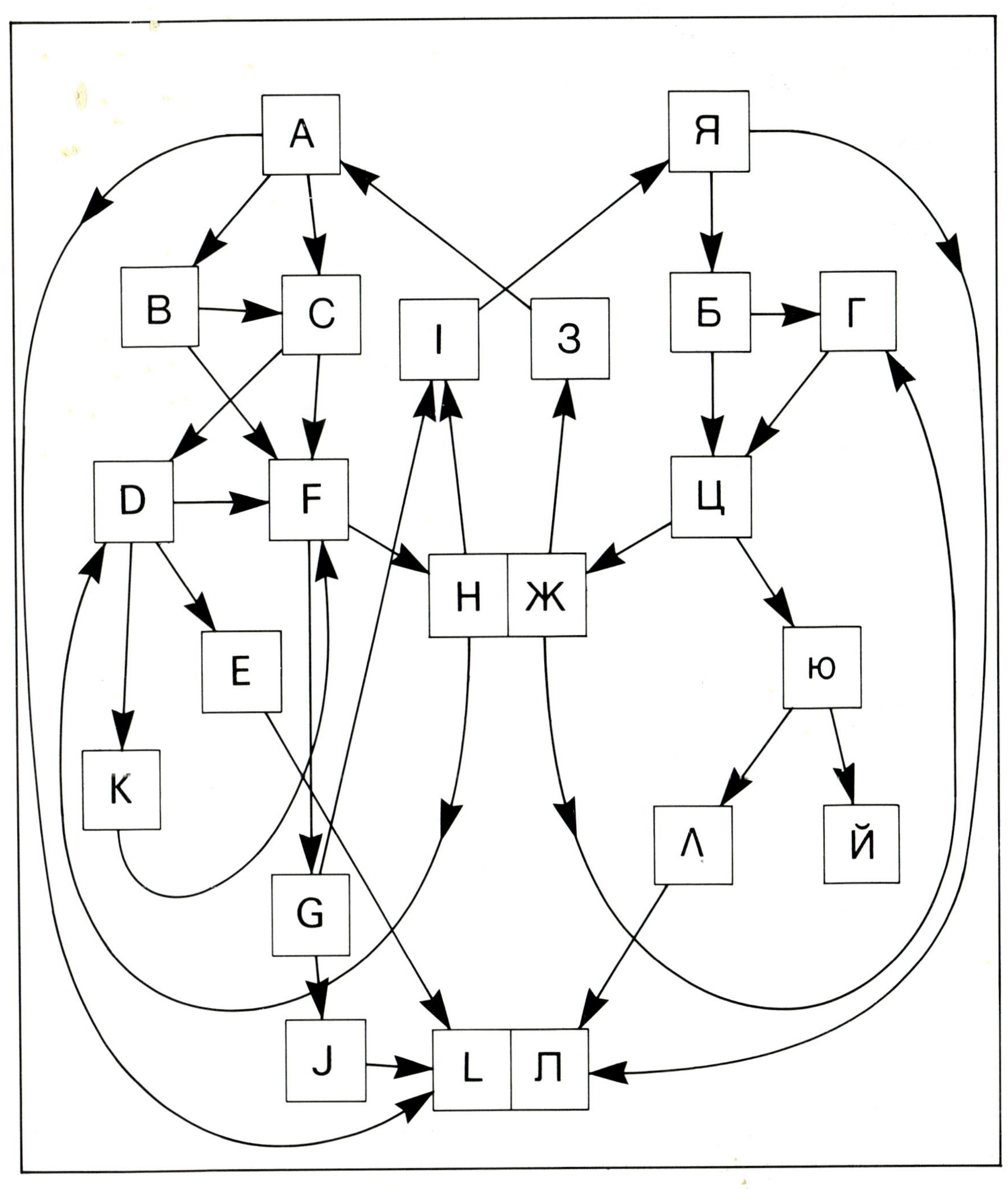

LEAK FROM

RUPERT MURDOCH'S

DIARY.

SOURCE: LOVEBAN

...o put my head between them & go "Flubalubalub". But ... let me. I give her the sack. Better luck next time.

...EMBER 1985

Get into the office at 5-30 this morning. I reckon it's vital to start the day at the first whiff of the sparrow's fart. Nothing to do for the next 3½ hours as the building's deserted. Go out to buy a paper but get stopped by the Monopolies Commission.

<u>9-05</u> My new secretary, Mercy Dash, hasn't arrived yet.

<u>9-15</u> Meeting with my two aides, Loveban and Probe. They tell me there's a strike at the Times. The print unions are refusing to work with our new computerized typesetting technology. Don't the bastards realize in the time it takes them to correct one misprint, these machines can print 400? That's progress!

<u>10-00</u> My secretary still hasn't arrived.

<u>10-30</u> I hold a board meeting re my interest in Twentieth Century Fox (and I don't mean Samantha. What a beaut!). I tell them the four qualities we need in our films are: first, literary merit; second, sumptuous camerawork; and third equal, tits. I send the boys away for a quick J. Arthur and a think.

<u>11-17</u> My secretary finally arrives. I give her the sack. Her tits are too small.

<u>11-35</u> The boys come back with a few film ideas: "2010 Tits – The year we make contact", "Bra-zil", "Titty Heat" and "Paris, Tits-ass". Probe suggests an adaptation of Hugo's "Les Miserables". I say, let's find out Hugo's surname before we commit ourselves. I leave early to find my new secretary, Dawn Raid.

<u>11-43</u> Dawn arrives. Give her the sack. She's wearing clothes.

12-15 Strike at the Sun. The journos are refusing to abandon obsolete technology, things like adjectives, adverbs & subordinate clauses. It looks like we're up Diarrhoea Gully in a lace canoe until Loveloan reminds me they wrote this week's news on Sunday. I celebrate by sacking them.

12-30 to 1-30 Working lunch - sacking the canteen staff.

3-05 Probe comes in to tell me Hugo's name is his surname and his first name is Victor. Luckily he seems to be a stiff, which solves the problem of who to make the cheques to. Good bloke, Probe.

4-00 More ideas. This time for musicals - "Paint Your Tits", "Titty Titty Bang Bang" and "14 Tits For 7 Brothers".

4-15 Still toying with the idea of a London evening paper. As it's like the Sun, but coming out in the evening, I decide to call it the Moon. That way we can print Samantha Fox's buttocks on the masthead.

5-30 More film titles: "Bonk With a Stranger", "Bra Busters", and "Beverly Hills Cup". Probe says the last one will have to be 3-D. 38-D more like. Beverly's a big girl! Loveloan suggests: "Twelve Angry Men" starring the ex-editors of my newspapers. We have a good laugh over this one before I sack him.

5-45 Strike at the News of the World. George Best's ex-girlfriends are seeking parity with the sex-change vicars.

6-00 I'm getting a real hard-on over this new evening paper. It's just the sort of tatty sensationalist rag London's been crying out for. Then I realize the Standard's beaten us to it. Get the drop.

6-30 Probe calls me about the "Les Miserables" project. Jeremy Irons will play the part of Les. I think Probe's really showing talent and initiative. I sack him.

7-15 As another day ends for News International and I give the night cleaners their cards, I wonder what tomorrow will hold for me and my loyal gang of workers. Then I remember. There aren't any left. Work-shy bastards!

Reader's Disgust

The Reader's Disgust Association Limited
25 Burkeley Square,
London W1X 6AB

Dear Mr. Robert Runcie of Cathedral Drive, Canterbury

Here is an offer that can bring you eternal salvation as well as your own copy of the new READER'S DISGUST Condensed Bible! Yes, Robert Runcie , you are one of the Chosen People (in Cathedral Drive, Canterbury) to receive news of this marvellous saver of time and souls! Just think, Robert , the READER'S DISGUST Condensed Bible offers you a short cut to Paradise by leaving out all the dull and obscure bits like:

	IN	OUT
Obadiah		X
Nahum		X
Haggai		X
Malachi		X
Habakkuk		X

Forget them, Robert Runcie !! The READER'S DISGUST Condensed Bible sticks to tried and tested ingredients. Your old favourites in a condensed form !!!

We have

- **Excerpts from Exodus**
- **Parts of Proverbs**
- **Psnippets from Psalms**
- **A morsel of Matthew**
- **A tad of Timothy**
- **A peek at Peter.**

How could you refuse, Bob ?

PLUS!!! MOSES' TOP TEN TIPS FOR KEEPING OUT OF TROUBLE.
AND!!! SOLOMON'S SAUCY SONG. (It's all right! They were married!)

ALSO!!! ENTERTAINING AND ABSORBING ARTICLES INCLUDING:-

- It Pays to Increase Your Prayer Power
- The moving story of how reformed murderer Samson coped with his blindness to become an entertainer who brought the house down.
- £75 for your letters that tell the funny side of everyday life beyond the Veil—The After-life's Like That.
- The hilarious adventures of the Assyrian Army—Humour in Cuneiform.
- The story of Salome—I Am John's Head.

Yes, Runcie-boy, forget those "begats"!!!! Send off *now* from Cathedral Drive, Canterbury for the READER'S DISGUST Condensed Bible! Just cut out the YES! coupon, post it to us with the form and get the Book FREE!! And if you don't want to pay after 14 DAYS, you can pay in the After-life. Go on! Do it! You won't be sorry, Robert Runcie! What's keeping you? Send it off now, for Christ's sake!!!

Each volume features:

- Miracle™ quality wipe-clean flexi-covers
- 125 full-colour illuminations
- 120 'Quotable Quotes' underlined in red
- 37 pages

Other titles in this series:

The Kompressed Koran
The Tightened Talmud
The Veri-Short Veda

I agree to eternal salvation and perpetual bliss in the world beyond. If I am not entirely satisfied after 2 weeks I may cancel my order with no loss whatsoever.

No, thank you

I wish to be consigned into everlasting damnation and suffer the barbs and flames of the Abyss. I realize, however, that I retain the right to claim my free READER'S DISGUST clip on reading lamp.

Mr/Mrs/Miss/Rev ....

Address ....

Town/Diocese ....

Postcode ....

Please sign ....

I believe in the physical Resurrection.

Try your skills with....

MAGGIE'S PUZZLE PAGE

PARTY LINES

See if you can re-draw the boundaries of these constituencies so as to leave a Tory MP in each one

RIDDLE-ME-REE!

Q: Why did the chicken cross the road?
A: *To get out of a Labour-controlled Authority.*

Q: What's black and white and red all over?
A: *The Guardian.*

Q: How many pinkos can you fit in a jail ?
A: *As many as you like.*

Q: What has 48 legs and an IQ of 170?
A: *My cabinet.*

Q: When is a chair not a chair?
A: *Just after Willie's sat on it.*

Q: What's brown, runny and smells?
A: *Gummer's nose.*

Q: If an unemployed school leaver jumps from the eighth floor, and a pensioner jumps from the fifth floor three seconds later, who reaches the ground first?
A: *Who cares?*

Teacher: Why haven't you done your homework?
Boy: *I can't afford the books!*

Join the dots

Well, that was fun, wasn't it?

SPOT THE DIFFERENCE

Here's a typical British scene for you to colour in.
1. rosy *2*. rosy *3*. rosy *4*. gold *5*. white
6. blue *7*. pinko *8*. black

A-MAZING!

See if you can help Nigel find his arse!

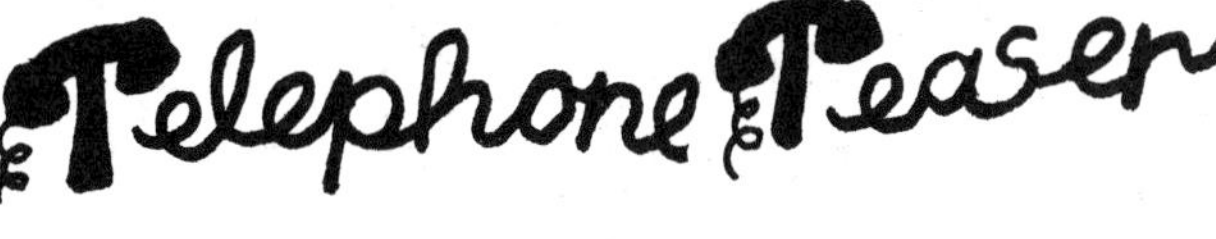

Who are the subversives talking to?
Follow the wires to find out!

And, finally, solve this puzzle to discover Maggie's hidden manifesto!

NEXT YEAR'S

JANUARY

The sale of Harrods to an Arab consortium completed when the new owners take possession of the building by slipping it under their robes.

After complaints from the Advertising Standards Authority, the Sinclair C5 is renamed "The Sinclair Walk-Car".

To equal the success of British Film Year, 1986 is designated Lebanese Architecture Year.

FEBRUARY

The Government announces that it created a record number of small businesses last year, including British Steel, the NCB and British Aerospace.

Millions of pounds are poured into a computerised screening campaign against cervical cancer after someone convinces Kenneth Clark that men can get it too.

One of the lucky ones! Ex-Youth Training Scheme teenager, Dean Harris (right), settles down to his new life as a plough.

MARCH

The chairman of the NCB, Mr Ian MacGregor, is to close down Lord Whitelaw's trousers on the grounds that the seams are exhausted.

Composer Andrew Lloyd-Webber and his lovely wife, Sara Brightman, listen to the first playback of his new Requiem.

APRIL

At a press conference in Washington, President Reagan admits that he is planning another Vietnam in Central America. But, he adds, only if he can persuade the French to go in first.

As new measures are introduced to prevent dogs fouling the high streets, Madonna's records are withdrawn from the shops.

MAY

The report by medical experts confirming that an apple a day really does keep the doctor away has caused David Owen to be inundated with boxes of Golden Delicious.

Privatisation works! Pensioner, Mr Joe Chudleigh, 68, takes advantage of Hereford's new deregulated bus service.

NEWS

JUNE

The Government announces a tenfold reduction in the unemployment figures. This has been achieved by knocking one of the noughts off the end.

The crew of the Challenger Shuttle returns to Earth with several samples of space rock. A disappointed President Reagan comments: "I've looked at every piece and none of them has 'SPACE' written all the way through."

The Bishop of Durham undergoes the Government's latest episcopal vetting procedure.

JULY

The England cricket team's plans to celebrate their Test series victory over India are cancelled when nobody can remember what to do.

No class distinctions here. Mirror Group publisher, Robert Maxwell, exchanges a quip with attendant Alf Green in the new lift at Maxwell House.

AUGUST

The Department of Transport says it has received no objections to the extension of Stansted airport. A spokesman denies that this is because all letters of complaint are sorted by the Heathrow baggage handlers.

SEPTEMBER

Following the introduction of admission charges to museums it now costs £3.50 to get into the Mike Yarwood show.

Thanks, suckers! Small investor, Pamela Robertson-Smythe of Esher, rearranges her mantelpiece after selling her shares in British Telecom.

OCTOBER

Anti-birth control campaigner Victoria Gillick claims that the majority of Britons are on her side. "I should know," she adds, "I am their mother."

NOVEMBER

Sir Clive Sinclair announces a new micro-computer, the Sinclair QL Plus. When asked to describe it, he says, "It's the Sinclair QL plus a set of tumblers when you buy it."

DECEMBER

The formalities of handing Hong Kong over to its rightful owners begin with the return of the Police Force to the Triad.

MICHAEL GRADE

We regret that the send-up of Michael Grade planned for this page was so popular and successful that he has decided to axe it.

A LIFE IN THE DAY OF DENNIS SKINNER – THE BEAST OF BOLSOVER

ONE-MAN-BANNED FROM THE COMMONS

I generally wake up around 7.00 a.m. This is when the wife throws me out of bed. Then there's time for a quick skim through the Tory media to find out what lies they're telling about me. According to the Express today my breakfast consists of middle-class children, so just to prove them wrong I make do with a bacon butty.

I don't have much time for fancy clothes. This is because I'm usually thrown out of the house before I've a chance to finish dressing. But, of course, a red tie is essential – in fact I'd feel naked without it. If it's a very bad day I am naked without it.

The bus ride to Westminster is quite a lengthy one, particularly as I have to keep arguing with the conductor to allow me back on, but

before long I'm standing before the Palace of Westminster, arguing with the doorman. Sometimes my suspension's been a long one, so he doesn't recognise me and won't let me in. But more often than not he does recognise me and throws me out.

However, once I'm inside the hallowed House of Commons I get down to the serious task of representing the needs of ordinary working people – by annoying Roy Jenkins. There are several effective ways of doing this. One is to plaster the Members' notice board with photos of him with targets drawn over his face. Another is to make claret jokes in a very loud voice. But my personal favourite is to knock on his office door and run away before he has the chance to open it.

You see, the problem with this place is that they care more about tradition than about ordinary people. Any breach of etiquette is reckoned to be "unparliamentary". So you can decimate the National Health Service, you can close down the coal industry, but you can't fill David Owen's brogues with itching powder without them showing you the door.

And once you get a name for it the authorities never forget. One day I put my feet up on the SDP bench and the next time they touched the ground was when I was washed ashore at Deptford.

Still, I've had a good run latel I've even managed to use the cantee a couple of times thanks to a hook- beard I've borrowed from Heffer.

I spend the evenings dealing w constituency work, writing pa phlets, or tying doorknockers together in Belgravia. Then it's time for the long slog home before settling down for the night on the sofa in the lounge. Just as I am drifting off to the land of Utopian dreams the cat throws me off.

A LIFE IN THE DAY OF JUNIOR DEFENCE MINISTER JOHN STANLEY

...AND STATISTICS

I usually get up around 5 am because being a bachelor means I've just spent the night with Brigitte Bardot or Raquel Welch. Then I usually get up around 7.30 when the wife brings me a cup of tea. I take two papers – the Sun and the Daily Mail – as they're the only two that can match my own grasp of reality.

At 8 I drive the Jensen through an amazing car chase to the Ministry of Defence. Being Secretary of State means you're a man of dignity and importance, so if I'm with someone I want to impress I make sure the staff call me Mr Heseltine.

First off I spend a couple of hours opening letters – mostly addressed to Joan Ruddock or Tam Dalyell. Then it's time for my own correspondence. In my position you have to handle a lot of hate mail, but I try to get the bulk of it written by 11.

The rest of the morning will pass in a variety of ways – wrestling with anacondas in the Brazilian jungle – saving the world from alien invasion – or, if I really feel like escaping into the realms of fantasy, I'll answer a few parliamentary questions.

After lunch – I usually go to Burger King (Home of the Whopper) – it's time to meet my constituents. Today some of them wanted to be shown round the Commons so I sent them a map of Tooting. Then it's off home and if the bus is on time I make a mental note to prosecute the timetable.

When I get in I play three concurrent games of grandmaster blindfold chess with my three children – George Michael of Wham!, Tracey Ullman and Prince William. Then I join my wife – no, Chrissie Brinkley – for a candle-lit dinner on the patio overlooking the Bay of Naples.

Just before I slip between the cover-ups I check my profile in the bathroom mirror – Pinocchio may be only a story but truth is sometimes stranger – well – just a stranger.

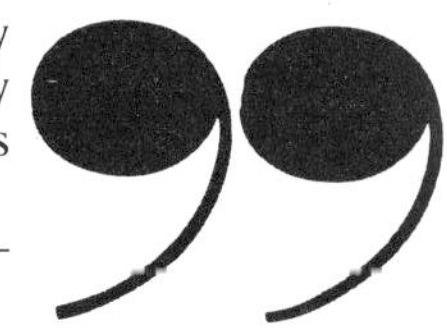

Next week: Walter Mitty